SUCCESS ON YOUR KNEES:

*A Seven Month Devotional
For Entrepreneurs*

Linda J. Williams

Annie Jean
Publishing, Inc.

Deer Park, New York

ISBN: 979-8-9889736-1-4
Library of Congress Number: 2023920569

Printed in the U.S.A.

Published by Annie Jean Publishing, Inc.
Deer Park, New York 11729
www.anniejeanpublishing@gmail.com

Dedication Page

First and foremost, I dedicate this book to God my Father, who provided every word that I have written.

I would also like to dedicate this book to my grandchildren, Anella and Eli Morton, and to all grandchildren and generations that come after them. Always remember to seek the Lord in all things, knowing that He will guide you into your purpose which is your passion. Never give up no matter how difficult it seems. This book is my testament to you of what God will do if you trust Him to guide you in His plan for your life.

Table of Contents

Foreword

"More than a devotional, it is a tool that all Christian business owners should read and apply to lead them to greater success in their business."

I have known Linda since 2010. As an etiquette officer, she has the gift of teaching courtesy from a godly perspective. As a business owner, Linda takes the skills she has learned to share with others to introduce business God's way.

"This book of the law....."

This is an amazing devotional for entrepreneurs, and one of the first of its kind. As an entrepreneur for over 20 years, and a Christian over 30, part of my quiet time with God includes prayer and reading my daily devotion. I would always pray for the success of my business utilizing scripture. But when it came to finding a devotional specific to business, it was a challenge until reading *Success on Your Knees.*

I congratulate Linda as she eloquently blended biblical principles with business knowledge and the result is *Success on Your Knees*. It is a devotional that inspires, challenges, and encourages all business owners. More specifically, it teaches us how to incorporate the Word of God into our business for success. Reading and applying this devotional will give you a totally new perspective on the business that God has blessed you with.

Elder Audrey Lewis, MA
Biblical Counselor and Entrepreneur

Introduction

Entrepreneurs should always be looking for new ways to make their business more successful. Whether it is a change in branding, an updated marketing campaign or a new product, we must constantly look for new ways to improve our business.

This book offers a strategy to change the way you do business. It may be new to some and a new level for others. I know it worked for me (and is still working), so I want to share it with you. It doesn't matter what your denomination is (or even if you are not religious), this strategy can work for you. Before you dismiss it as being whimsical or impractical, I challenge you to buy the book and take the time to read the daily devotions. Whether you are already successful, I believe that you will gain valuable insight about yourself, your business, and the divine power behind it.

My journey to write this book was quite unusual. July 2021, I was asked to take on the role of leader of the business ministry group in my church. Although I owned a consulting business for over 20 years, it was a small business. I didn't feel qualified to lead this group of startup entrepreneurs, but I followed the divine indication I was getting and accepted the assignment. After the first couple of months, hearing (and being able to identify with) the struggles of the group, I offered to send them a daily scripture with a word of encouragement, which they welcomed. About one year later, all ministry meetings were put on hold until the new year.

It was then that I understood that the devotions were my next book! When it was revealed it to me, I prayed about how many devotions there should be. The answer was seven months of devotions because that is the biblical number of completion. I was totally overwhelmed! I began to pray for direction for the format, which devotions to use, etc. The result is the book that you are holding in your hands.

If you are reading this, you have either decided to launch your business, or you already have an established business but realize that you still need direction. You may have done research, attended conferences or seminars on business and feel that you have done everything the experts suggested. You may have even prayed, but something is still missing. As I sit here on the beach (my favorite place to write), I remember the process of the development of my business. From becoming a certified etiquette consultant to a church etiquette consultant to an author to a certified book coach, I have come to understand who guides my business. I can honestly say I had the knowledge, skill, and passion for all these services, but did not know to see them as a business until I asked for spiritual insight.

I share my journey with you to let you know that I, as a Christian entrepreneur, march to a different drum and am held to a different and higher standard. Hopefully, every business owner feels that they have a gift or level of expertise for the product or service they offer to be successful financially, as the world's standards indicate. This book offers another level of entrepreneurship, that of understanding that your business was not just created for you to make money, but also to help others in a way that activates your purpose in life. We must understand that success is also measured by the lives we touch. When I felt like I wasn't successful because I wasn't making a ton of money, I asked myself, "What was I doing wrong?" When I realized that my primary motivation should be to help others, my financial situation changed. Our primary focus is God's purpose, not financial gain. When we follow our heart and His direction, we will truly be successful.

This is a seven-month daily devotional. The devotions are a result of fasting, prayer, Bible study, godly counsel, and my experience as a Christian in business. Regardless of what stage your business is in, there will be times of frustration, discouragement, successes, and lessons to be learned. This devotional provides scriptures, practical commentaries, and an opportunity for you to meditate and write down your thoughts each day. It is a progression of four phases; *Breaking of the Old, Letting Go, Planting & Cultivating, and Walking in Newness.* You may see some scriptures more than once but in a different context. This is not redundant but intentional. All scriptures are taken from the Holy Bible, Holman Christian Standard Version unless otherwise noted.

At the end of the seven months, through prayer, Bible study, and application, you can be better equipped spiritually to reach the heights the Lord wants to take you to. You can begin your seven-month journey at any time. Be persistent, consistent, and have faith. Do not neglect the structure, skills, marketing, education, and other aspects that are necessary for a successful business, but put this seven-month commitment at the forefront of your priorities. If you do this, I believe that you will see a difference in your business and your life.

1ˢᵗ Phase – Breaking of the Old

Breaking or changing any behavior or habits that have become a part of your personality can be difficult. Your resistance to being broken can be due to ignorance (not knowing that you are disobeying God's commands); unwillingness to let go of a habit, attitude, or desire that you know is wrong; or perhaps you are running from the call on your life. You must make up your mind, once and for all, who will be in control of your life, you, or God?

In this "1ˢᵗ Phase" of devotions, we will be looking at who we have become as opposed to who God wants us to be. We will honestly look at what needs breaking in our minds, hearts, and lives. We will focus on scriptures that will teach us how to begin the breaking process. The scriptures in this phase can help you to grow in the Lord.

1. Take a Look in the Mirror

Good morning entrepreneurs,

For now, we see indistinctly, as in a mirror, but then face to face. Now I know in part, but then I will know fully, as I am fully known (I Corinthians 13:12).

COMMENTARY

As we begin this journey, take a few minutes to reflect on what God has brought you through, this year and years before, in your business and your personal life. Then rejoice that God kept His hand on you! God bless.

Write one significant thing God has brought you through in the past year (be specific).

_____

_____

_____

_____

_____

_____

_____

_____

_____

_____

_____

2. What Does Your Reflection Look Like to Others?

Good morning entrepreneurs,

Summing it all up, friends, I'd say you'll do best by filling your minds and meditating on things true, noble, reputable, authentic, compelling, gracious—the best, not the worst; the beautiful, not the ugly; things to praise, not things to curse. Put into practice what you learned from me, what you heard, saw and realized. Do that, and God, who makes everything work together, will work you into his most excellent harmonies (Philippians 4:8-9 MSG Bible).

COMMENTARY

As you move into your next season, it is important to know there is a decorum (state of behavior, dignity, order), which we must carry ourselves as godly entrepreneurs. In addition, people form an impression of us within five seconds of seeing us, based on what we are wearing, what we say, our facial expression, and how we respond. We do not have a second chance to make a good first impression. Each time you get dressed to go out, take a look in the mirror. Do you look like an entrepreneur of God? Walk, talk, and dress with the decorum of God's entrepreneurs! God bless

Write what God revealed to you through today's devotion

_____

_____

_____

_____

_____

_____

_____

3. The Breaking Process

Good morning entrepreneurs,

Turn away from evil and do what is good; seek peace and pursue it (Psalm 34:14).

COMMENTARY

Spend time with God today asking Him to show you what things you need to "get right" in your life. As you focus on giving those things to God so He can break you and mold you into His image, you will see peace manifest itself in every area of your life. You will be silent about things you once had to have an opinion on. One big lesson I have learned is to be quiet, and let God do your talking in difficult situations and relationships. Peace CAN rule your life, but you must allow it (Philippians 4:7). God bless.

What specific habits or situations does God need to break you of (be very specific)

_____

_____

_____

_____

_____

_____

_____

_____

_____

4. In What Direction are You Going?

Good morning entrepreneurs,

No, we neither make nor save ourselves. God does both the making and saving. He creates each of us by Christ Jesus to join him in the work he does, the good work he has gotten ready for us to do, work we had better be doing (Ephesians 2:10 MSG Bible).

COMMENTARY

Each year should begin with prayerfully planning and creating two documents; (1) Vision Board, and (2) Yearly Plan. Without written God-directed plans, we don't know what we are doing for the year, nor do we know the steps to get there. Once God has guided you to complete the plans, ask Him for the steps to completion (He may not give you all the steps at once so be sure to complete each one). It's never too late to create your vision board! God bless.

Write what God revealed to you through today's devotion:

_____

_____

_____

_____

_____

_____

_____

_____

_____

5. Run the Race for Your Business

Good morning entrepreneurs,

Do you not know that those who run in a race all run, but only one receives the prize? Run in such a way that you may win (1 Corinthians 9:24 NASB).

COMMENTARY

Running a business is hard. It's a marathon not a sprint. There will be plenty of stumbling blocks in your way. Everyone trips and falls while running this race, but winners get up faster than everyone else. You must do what you need to do to win your race. Run your race for your business today! God bless.

Write what God revealed to you through today's devotion:

_____

_____

_____

_____

_____

_____

_____

_____

_____

_____

_____

6. Focus on What God CAN Do, Not What I CAN'T Do

Good morning entrepreneurs,

I can do all things through Him who strengthens me (Philippians 4:13 NASB).

COMMENTARY

Whenever you struggle with your self-confidence, read this bible verse. There will be times in your business when you need to force yourself to stretch beyond what you think is possible. I did it and so can you. You can do it. I believe in you, and God does too! God bless.

Write what God revealed to you through today's devotion:

_____

_____

_____

_____

_____

_____

_____

_____

_____

_____

_____

_____

7. What are You Afraid of?

Good morning entrepreneurs,
For God has not given us a spirit of [a]timidity, but of power and love and discipline. (2 Timothy 1:7 NASB).

COMMENTARY

Fear is the enemy of entrepreneurship. God wants us to go out with the power He gives us to pursue our business ideas. We may not want to admit it, but fear of failure (or success) can keep us from moving forward in the business for which God has given us the vision. Step out and move forward in Jesus's Name! Have a blessed day in the Lord. God bless.

Write what God revealed to you through today's devotion:

_____

_____

_____

_____

_____

_____

_____

_____

_____

_____

_____

8. How Long Do You Pray?

Good morning entrepreneurs,

Rejoice always, pray without ceasing, in everything give thanks; for this is the will of God for you in Christ Jesus (1 Thessalonians 5:16-18 NASB).

COMMENTARY

The most valuable thing you can do for your business is pray over it every day. You should thank God for the good days and bad days because bad days are just learning opportunities that help us appreciate good ones. Remember to give thanks to God for the gift of being blessed with the idea for a business today and every day! Have a wonderfully blessed day in the Lord today.

Write a brief prayer that you can pray each day for your business.

_____

_____

_____

_____

_____

_____

_____

_____

_____

_____

9. We are in This Together

Good morning entrepreneurs,

And let us consider [thoughtfully] how we may encourage one another to love and to do good deeds, not forsaking our meeting together [as believers for worship and instruction], as is the habit of some, but encouraging one another; and all the more [faithfully] as you see the day [of Christ's return] approaching (Hebrews 10:24-25 Amplified Version).

COMMENTARY

We must make the time to encourage other entrepreneurs. Sometimes we all get busy, but don't ever be too busy to share, inspire, mentor, or be a sounding board for another business owner. It's a heavy burden we carry as owners, and we all need to remember we are not alone. Look for spiritually grounded entrepreneur groups, join organizations in your industry, attend conferences (virtual and in-person). Be strategic, connect with conferences and opportunities to gather with other godly entrepreneurs because we understand the unique struggles we face and can encourage each other. God bless.

Search on the internet or contact someone today to connect with a group of religious entrepreneurs. Write down the names, emails, and phone numbers below.

_____

_____

_____

_____

_____

_____

10. God's Got You!

Good morning entrepreneurs,
I am sure of this, that he who started a good work in you will carry it on to completion until the day of Christ Jesus (Philippians 1:6).

COMMENTARY

Always remember God's covering. He will seed you with ideas, and rest assured, He never gives you a plan that you don't have the inner strength and ability to execute. He also will send you all the help you need. We all need to stay humble and accept help when it comes. Change begins with the DECISION to change.

What did God reveal to you through today's devotion:

_____

_____

_____

_____

_____

_____

_____

_____

_____

_____

_____

_____

11. Move When God Says Move

Good morning entrepreneurs,

And our people must also learn to devote themselves to good works for cases of urgent need, so that they will not be unfruitful (Titus 3:14).

COMMENTARY

God will help us to build our business, but we must move when He tells us. If you do nothing, nothing will happen. He can put a business dream in your heart, but He won't make you pursue it. He can connect you with someone knowledgeable in an area you are struggling in, but He won't make you ask for help because He gives us free will. Focus each day being productive and purposeful. Seek His guidance on ways to learn, better yourself, and take action. God bless!

Do you hesitate to ask for help from godly people? Why?

_____

_____

_____

_____

_____

_____

_____

_____

_____

_____

12. Avoid the Discouraging Words

Good morning entrepreneurs,

Commit your way to the Lord; trust in Him, and He will act, making your righteousness shine like the dawn, your justice like the noonday (Psalm 37:5-6).

COMMENTARY

No one can stop God's anointing. There will be times in your life when people will try to discourage you, telling you that you are wasting your time, or flat out telling you that you won't make it through. No one can stop God's anointing on your life. If He gave you the idea for your business, He will bless it. Stay faithful, maintain integrity, and focus on God's word and His promise. He can give you favor and open doors for you that appear impossible in the natural. God bless.

Think of some of the negative words people have spoken to you about your business. Now turn those words into positive ones!

_____

_____

_____

_____

_____

_____

_____

_____

_____

13. Passion Fuels Purpose

Good morning entrepreneurs,
Whatever you do, do it enthusiastically, as something done for the Lord and not for men (Colossians 3:23).

COMMENTARY

Do you have a passion for the business idea God has given you? Do you have a passion to do God's will? Passion is defined as "A strong or extravagant fondness, enthusiasm, or desire for anything" (Dictionary.com LLC). If you lack this enthusiasm for your business, you will lack motivation. You will discourage easily when things don't go the way you expect.

Ask God today to give you a greater passion for the business He has blessed you with so that you can share it with the world as He leads you so He will get the glory! God bless.

Write down what gives you the most excitement about your business.

_____

_____

_____

_____

_____

_____

_____

_____

14. A Lesson From the "Birds of the Air"

Good morning entrepreneurs,

Don't worry about anything, but in everything, through prayer and petition with thanksgiving, let your requests be made known to God. And the peace of God, which surpasses every thought, will guard your hearts and minds in Christ Jesus (Philippians 4:6-7).

COMMENTARY

Starting your business can be stressful. What do I do first? How can I find time to devote to my business? Is my product or service needed? What if someone else is already doing it? Where will I obtain the money that is needed? These and so many other questions go through our minds. We must remember to go to God with ALL questions about our business because He gave us the business and knows all things. He will answer or provide godly counsel to help us. Starting your business should not be stressful. Ask God to remove the stress and guide you through the exciting and amazing opportunity He has given you to serve Him and others. Let each day be a joyful journey to building your business! Like the birds of the air, allow God to guide you. Have a wonderfully blessed day in the Lord. God bless.

Ask God to show you the number one thing causing you stress about your business. Write it here, then pray and ask God to remove the stress you are feeling.

_____

_____

_____

_____

_____

15. Close Your Eyes and Cast Your Net

Good morning entrepreneurs,

As the crowd was pressing in on Jesus to hear God's word, He was standing by Lake Gennesaret. He saw two boats at the edge of the lake; the fishermen had left them and were washing their nets. He got into one of the boats, which belonged to Simon, and asked him to put out a little from the land. Then He sat down and was teaching the crowds from the boat.

When He had finished speaking, He said to Simon, "Put out into deep water and let down your nets for a catch." "Master," Simon replied, "We've worked hard all night long and caught nothing! But at Your word, I'll let down the nets." When they did this, they caught a great number of fish, and their nets began to tear. So, they signaled to their partners in the other boat to come and help them; they came and filled both boats so full that they began to sink (Luke 5:1-7).

COMMENTARY

Don't move based on what your eyes see; move based on what God tells you to do for your business. When you begin to do that, your net will overflow with opportunity. Have a wonderfully blessed day in the Lord! God bless.

Has God shown you where to cast your net? What were the results?

_____

_____

_____

_____

_____

_____

_____

16. Don't Look Down

Good morning entrepreneurs,

Immediately He made the disciples get into the boat and go ahead of Him to the other side, while He dismissed the crowds. After dismissing the crowds, He went up on the mountain by Himself to pray. When evening came, He was there alone. But the boat was already over a mile from land, battered by the waves, because the wind was against them. Around three in the morning, He came toward them walking on the sea. When the disciples saw Him walking on the sea, they were terrified. "It's a ghost!" they said and cried out in fear. Immediately Jesus spoke to them. "Have courage! It is I. Don't be afraid." "Lord, if it's You," Peter answered Him, "Command me to come to You on the water." "Come!" He said. And climbing out of the boat, Peter started walking on the water and came toward Jesus (Matthew 14:22-29).

COMMENTARY

Have courage! Have faith! When God tells you to get out of the boat and do something new regarding your business, trust the Lord and "walk on the water" because Jesus is there to navigate the way and keep you from sinking. God bless.

What is one thing that is keeping you from "getting out of the boat?"

_____

_____

_____

_____

_____

_____

17. Are You a Jabez?

Good morning entrepreneurs,
Jabez called out to the God of Israel: "If only You would bless me, extend my border, let Your hand be with me, and keep me from harm, so that I will not cause any pain." And God granted his request (1Chronicles 4:10).

COMMENTARY

I prayed this prayer daily for years (and still pray it) that the Lord would enlarge my territory to give me opportunities to reach and bless people all over the world through my business, and He has done that. As a result of a family trip to Ghana, I connected with a publisher and writer looking to publish her book. You have no idea how God will enlarge your territory until you ask Him! Have a blessed day in the Lord.

How has God enlarged your territory? How would you like Him to allow it in the future?

_____

_____

_____

_____

_____

_____

_____

_____

_____

_____

18. Give Thanks to God for Your Business

Good morning entrepreneurs,
Come, let us worship and bow down; let us kneel before the Lord our Maker (Psalm 95:6).

COMMENTARY

Because God made us, He knows all about us and how He wants us to use the gifts He has given us. It is a blessing to be given the gift of a business ministry. Worship and thank God for the opportunity to be used by Him for your unique business! God bless.

What is your specific gift that launched/ignited your business? How did God reveal it to you?

_____

_____

_____

_____

_____

_____

_____

_____

_____

_____

_____

_____

19. Identifying Your Gift

Good morning entrepreneurs,

And He personally gave some to be apostles, some prophets, some evangelists, some pastors, and teachers, for the training of the saints in the work of ministry, to build up the body of Christ (Ephesians 4:11-12).

COMMENTARY

God's unique gift, that is in each of us, is to be used to save souls and enlighten believers in the church, in our business, and in the world. You have been blessed with a business, which gives you special opportunities to use your gift to touch and save lives; don't miss them. God bless.

How do you make sure to use your gift to touch lives each day?

_____

_____

_____

_____

_____

_____

_____

_____

_____

_____

_____

20. Releasing Your Gift to God

Good morning entrepreneurs,

A man's gift maketh room for him, and bringeth him before great men (Proverbs 18:16 KJV).

COMMENTARY

God made us each uniquely and differently. When we consider our purpose, it should match who we are. It may not even be something that we like to do, and that is what makes it God's gift. Other people see it in you, but you see it as something that is not your strength. Guess what? It is not YOUR strength, but God giving you the strength to use the gift for His purpose for you. To do that, you must give it back to the Lord! Don't hold on to it trying to improve it. It is only by releasing your gift to God that He can then use it through you for His glory. God bless.

Have you released your gift to God? How can you begin to do that today?

_____

_____

_____

_____

_____

_____

_____

_____

_____

21. The Possibility of the Impossible

Good morning entrepreneurs,

But Jesus looked at them and said, "With men this is impossible, but with God all things are possible" (Matt 19:26).

COMMENTARY

The things that you don't plan for are the things that can open you to opportunities and blessings you never thought possible. In Colin Powell's *13 Rules of Leadership*, rule # 4 is, "It can be done." The success of your business may seem impossible with all the work and steps involved, but it can be done! Prayerfully make a weekly "To Do List" (which coincides with your vision board) and complete those items weekly. Building a business is like building a structure, one brick at a time! Trust God and watch the impossible become possible. God bless.

Begin your change by creating a "To Do List" today. If you already have these lists, review them, and write below how you can be more strategic about completing them.

_____

_____

_____

_____

_____

_____

_____

_____

22. Give, Then Receive

Good morning entrepreneurs,

Give, and it will be given to you. They will pour into your lap a good measure—pressed down, shaken together, and running over [with no space left for more]. For with the standard of measurement you use [when you do good to others], it will be measured to you in return (Luke 6:38 AMP).

COMMENTARY

The primary motivation for a godly person in business must be to serve, help, and be a blessing to others. Sometimes people will need your services but cannot pay or cannot pay full price. Prayerfully develop a fee structure. The Holy Spirit will tell you when to charge and what to charge in each situation. Your obedience will result in blessings you never imagined. It is not just about money; referrals, connections, and wisdom will also result. When the primary goal is to bless others, your business will be successful beyond measure. God bless.

What is one thing that you can do to be a bigger blessing to others through your business?

_____

_____

_____

_____

_____

_____

_____

23. The Blessing of Being Generous

Good morning entrepreneurs,
A generous person will be enriched, and the one who gives a drink of water will receive water (Proverbs 11:25).

COMMENTARY

It's nice to be seen, but it's nicer to help someone else to be seen. One of the blessings of knowledge and growing is that you can help and be a resource for someone else to grow. Take every opportunity to reach back and give assistance to others when God provides the opportunity. Doing so will give you unspeakable joy as you watch them grow. God bless.

What did God reveal to you through today's devotion?

_____

_____

_____

_____

_____

_____

_____

_____

_____

_____

_____

24. Real Faith or Implied Faith

Good morning entrepreneurs,

Now faith is the assurance (title deed, confirmation) of things hoped for (divinely guaranteed), and the evidence of things not seen [the conviction of their reality—faith comprehends as fact what cannot be experienced by the physical senses] (Hebrews 11:1).

COMMENTARY

How strongly do you believe in your business? Do you have faith that it will exist and be successful? To answer these questions requires a deeper understanding of faith. "What is faith?" It is confidence that someone or something is reliable. Our whole life is based on faith. Without it, banks and post offices would not be possible. Paper money and credit cards would never be accepted (the very word credit is from the Latin verb "to believe How diligently (persistently) are you seeking (asking God for guidance) for your business?" (Nelson's Foundational Bible Dictionary, 2004).

The importance of having faith to believe can hardly be overstated: *But without faith it is impossible to please Him, for he who comes to God must believe that He is, and that He is a rewarder of those who diligently seek Him* [Hebrews 11:6] (Nelson's Foundational Bible Dictionary, 2004). God bless.

What did God reveal to you through today's devotion?

_____

_____

_____

_____

_____

25. Written Plan or Verbal Plan, What Really Works?

Good morning entrepreneurs,

And then God answered: "Write this. Write what you see. Write it out in big block letters so that it can be read on the run. This vision-message is a witness pointing to what's coming. It aches for the coming—it can hardly wait! And it doesn't lie. If it seems slow in coming, wait. It's on its way. It will come right on time" (Habakkuk 2:2-3 MSG).

COMMENTARY

Write out the vision of your business in a business plan. Also, keep a journal for your business so that you can record and remember the journey of building your business. Journaling can also help you in tracking your business and making necessary adjustments for growth. God bless.

Write down one specific vision God has given you for your business, then thank Him for it.

_____

_____

_____

_____

_____

_____

_____

_____

_____

_____

26. The Benefits of Fear

Good morning entrepreneurs,

Do not fear, for I am with you; do not be afraid, for I am your God. I will strengthen you; I will help you; I will hold on to you with My righteous right hand (Isaiah 41:10).

COMMENTARY

How you conquer fear? Each time the Holy Spirit gives you a thought or an idea, do it. When you see how God guided you to be successful, it will boost your faith. The song "Yield Not to Temptation" by H.R. Palmer has a line that says, "Each victory will help you some other to win." Each time you step out of your comfort zone and do what the Lord directs, you will gain confidence for the next assignment. So, what are you waiting for? Let your faith be bigger than your fear! God bless.

What did God reveal to you through today's devotion?

_____

_____

_____

_____

_____

_____

_____

_____

_____

27. The Conquest of YOUR Jericho

Good morning entrepreneurs,

Read Joshua 6:15-27 "The Conquest of Jericho"

COMMENTARY

Minister Qiana Hobdy preached a sermon at Friendship Baptist Church, Roslyn, NY titled, "A Voice Activated Victory" (see citation below). It is so relative to us as entrepreneurs. Joshua 6 is the story about how God led the Israelites to tear down the walls of Jericho and take possession of the land He promised them. To do it, they had to march around the wall seven times then shout!

As you read the scripture, listen for God to show you the walls standing in the way of your business. "You will have what you say you will have." Activate God's promises for your business by speaking to them out loud. Please take the time to listen to the sermon, Friendship Baptist Church, "A Voice Activated Victory", Facebook, December 12, 2021. It will inspire you to tear down the walls and activate God's promises for your business in the name of Jesus! God bless.

What did God reveal to you through today's devotion?

_____

_____

_____

_____

_____

_____

_____

28. God's Strength Comes First Not Last

Good morning entrepreneurs,

Finally, be strengthened by the Lord and by His vast strength (Ephesians 6:10).

COMMENTARY

Allow the Lord to empower you with His strength to do what is necessary in your business. No matter how difficult the task, the enormity of it is in your mind; God has already given you the strength and the tools to achieve it. God bless.

What did God reveal to you through today's devotion?

_____

_____

_____

_____

_____

_____

_____

_____

_____

_____

_____

_____

_____

29. Do You Want to Be Sent?

Good morning entrepreneurs,
Then I heard the voice of the Lord saying: "Who should I send? Who will go for Us?" I said: "Here I am. Send me" (Isaiah 6:8).

COMMENTARY

I was recently led by the Holy Spirit to volunteer to help with a job which involved using the gifts God has blessed me with. I was obedient even though I knew it would involve a lot of time. It took one month to complete the job but, doing it prayerfully gave me joy through the difficulty.

Starting a business is hard work, but the joy you feel as you use your gifts will override the difficulty involved. No matter what tasks you are given that involve using your gifts as you build your business, be willing to say, "Yes, I will do it Lord. Send me." Keep moving forward. God bless.

What did God reveal to you about accepting difficult jobs or those you feel inadequate for? How will you respond?

_____

_____

_____

_____

_____

_____

_____

30. Let God Speak for You

Good morning entrepreneurs,
Now then go, and I, even I, will be with your mouth, and will teach you what you shall say (Exodus 4:12 AMP).

COMMENTARY

Just like Moses (who stuttered when he spoke), there are times when we are hesitant to speak for fear of saying the wrong thing or not saying it in an eloquent manner. We miss opportunities to attend events where we could gain information or meet influential people who can help us. We avoid opportunities to speak about our business because we lack godly confidence.

When God gives you opportunities to speak about your business, know that He will give you the words to say. Trust Him and say what God tells you to say when He tells you to say it. Always remember your words (positive or negative) have power! God bless.

What did God reveal to you through today's devotion?

_____

_____

_____

_____

_____

_____

_____

_____

31. Missed Opportunities

Good morning entrepreneurs,

I know your works. Because you have limited strength, have kept My word, and have not denied My name, look, I have placed before you an open door that no one is able to close (Revelation 3:8).

COMMENTARY

Don't be discouraged when you miss opportunities. If it is a door that God has opened for you, only He can close it. You may think you have missed the opportunity, but God may present it to you at a different time or in a different way. At the same time, God can close doors if we are not being obedient to His call. Don't keep waiting when God is telling you to move. Even if you don't feel ready, prayerfully move because God's timing is always perfect! God bless.

What did God reveal to you through today's devotion?

_____

_____

_____

_____

_____

_____

_____

_____

_____

_____

32. The Courage of Waiting

Good morning entrepreneurs,

Wait for the Lord; be strong and courageous. Wait for the Lord (Psalm 27:14).

COMMENTARY

It takes courage to wait on God (know the difference between waiting on God and procrastination). Don't make a move first then ask God to bless it. Waiting on God involves prayer, fasting, and sitting before the Lord with pen and paper. What you receive may not be what you asked for, but it may be the first step. You must follow God's instructions for the first step to your prayer before He leads you to the next step. Understand that waiting on God is not a passive state but an active one. God bless.

What business decision have you asked the Lord to help you with? Are you still waiting? What has He given you to do while waiting?

_____

_____

_____

_____

_____

_____

_____

_____

33. Don't forget to Glorify God

Good morning entrepreneurs,

Therefore, whether you eat or drink, or whatever you do, do everything for God's glory

(1 Corinthians 10:31).

COMMENTARY

When you have even the smallest success in your business, always give God the glory. The more you thank and glorify God, the more you help others to understand that your success is not by your hand but by God's. They will prayerfully seek God more and you will be blessed all the more. God bless.

Write a specific success that that happened in your business and details on what happened.

_____

_____

_____

_____

_____

_____

_____

_____

_____

_____

_____

34. The Concept of Spiritual Sight

Good morning entrepreneurs,
But if we hope for what we do not see, we eagerly wait for it with patience (Romans 8:25).

COMMENTARY

Wait expectantly and confidently on God. Even when it looks like things are standing still or about to fall apart, don't become frustrated. Remember, "Faith is the substance of things hoped for, the evidence of things not {yet} seen" (Hebrews 11:1). Don't give up and don't give in! Blessings seem to come at the very time you are about to give up! God bless.

What did God reveal to you through today's devotion?

_____

_____

_____

_____

_____

_____

_____

_____

_____

_____

_____

35. How Do You Measure Your Giving?

Good morning entrepreneurs,

Give, and it will be given to you; a good measure—pressed down, shaken together, and running over—will be poured into your lap. For with the measure you use, it will be measured back to you (Luke 6:38).

COMMENTARY

When you give, do you assess it? Do you give expecting something in return (tangible or intangible)? Do you only give to those you know? Do you evaluate a person's level of need before you give, or do you give as God leads? Look to give to someone who is not able to give back to you. They will be blessed and so will you! God bless.

What did God reveal to you through today's devotion?

_____

_____

_____

_____

_____

_____

_____

_____

_____

_____

36. Are You Walking in God's Plans or Yours?

Good morning entrepreneurs,
"For I know the plans I have for you"—this is the Lord's declaration— "plans for your welfare, not for disaster, to give you a future and a hope" (Jeremiah 29:11).

COMMENTARY

Don't ask God to bless YOUR plans for your business; ask God what HIS plans are for your business, then obediently follow each step as He shows you. God bless.

What did God reveal to you through today's devotion?

_____

_____

_____

_____

_____

_____

_____

_____

_____

_____

_____

_____

_____

37. Go! Opportunities to Share God's Word

Good morning entrepreneurs,

Go, therefore, and make disciples of all nations, baptizing them in the name of the Father and of the Son and of the Holy Spirit, teaching them to observe everything I have commanded you. And remember, I am with you always, to the end of the age (Matt 28:19-20).

COMMENTARY

As godly entrepreneurs, we must use the gifts God has enabled and blessed us with to teach and share with others, so that they may see the Spirit of God in us through our gifts and have a desire to give their lives to Christ. The gift of our business is not just to have a business, but to provide another means for us to share the gospel of Jesus Christ. God bless.

What did God reveal to you through today's devotion?

_____

_____

_____

_____

_____

_____

_____

_____

_____

_____

38. The Importance of Protecting Your Heart

Good morning entrepreneurs,

Guard your heart above all else, for it is the source of life (Proverbs 4:23).

COMMENTARY

Know the boundaries (of your heart, soul, principles, beliefs); where your boundaries end and someone else's begins. Don't allow others to invade or change your boundaries. When you do, your heart becomes vulnerable. God's Word says to "Guard your heart." That means to protect it from hurt, pain and disappointment. You are responsible TO others, but you are also responsible FOR yourself and your heart. Keep those things (and people) who will nurture you close and avoid those who will not (2 Corinthians 6:11-14). God bless.

What did God reveal to you through today's devotion?

_____

_____

_____

_____

_____

_____

_____

_____

_____

_____

39. Be Careful of Detours

Good morning entrepreneurs,
He renews my life; He leads me along the right paths for His name's sake
(Psalm 23:3).

COMMENTARY

Trust God to keep you on your assigned journey. Be careful of detours that can derail you. If the way you are about to go into gives you cause for doubt, pause and wait on God's confirmation. Don't be afraid of missing an opportunity by pausing; God is always on time! God bless.

What did God reveal to you through today's devotion?

_____

_____

_____

_____

_____

_____

_____

_____

_____

_____

_____

_____

40. The Planting Process

Good morning entrepreneurs,

For now, we see indistinctly, as in a mirror, but then face to face. Now I know in part, but then I will know fully, as I am fully known (I Corinthians 13:12).

COMMENTARY

Take a few minutes to reflect on what God has brought you through in the last year and years before. Think about what He has done in your personal life and in your business. The trials and tribulations you experienced help to defeat the old you and mold the new you. You can look and see who you were and observe the "New You" in Christ. Periodically take time through each year to reflect on how God has changed you. Then rejoice that God kept His hand on you! God bless.

How has God changed you in the last year? Five years?

_____

_____

_____

_____

_____

_____

_____

_____

_____

_____

41. Choosing the Right Doors

Good morning entrepreneurs,

I know your works. Because you have limited strength, have kept My word, and have not denied My name, look, I have placed before you an open door that no one is able to close (Rev. 3:8).

COMMENTARY

We don't know what lies ahead, but we know as God's child, He said if we keep His commandments and do not deny His Name, He will open doors of opportunity for us that we are not strong or even wise enough to open. Be prayerful and discerning so that you do not miss those opportunities to grow your business, serve or minister. Only God knows what He will do for you in the future. God bless.

What did God reveal to you through today's devotion?

_____

_____

_____

_____

_____

_____

_____

_____

_____

_____

42. The Pathway to Success

Good morning entrepreneurs,

For nothing will be impossible with God (Luke 1:37).

COMMENTARY

The most difficult tasks and trials always seem so daunting when we are in the middle of them. It is only when we are on the other side that we can see the benefit of what we went through and how God brought us through. Lord, help us not to focus on the difficult tasks and trials in starting and running our business, but focus on how you strengthen and empower us through them so that we can serve others. If God is leading us, no matter how hard it seems or how fearful we are, remember NOTHING is impossible for God! God bless.

What daunting task are you facing today? Write it below then pray and ask God how to proceed.

_____

_____

_____

_____

_____

_____

_____

_____

_____

_____

43. Are You Anxious or Nervous?

Good morning entrepreneurs,

Be anxious for nothing, but in everything by prayer and supplication, with thanksgiving, let your requests be made known to God (Philippians 4:6 NKJV).

COMMENTARY

There is a difference between being anxious and being nervous, and it involves the intensity or degree of your emotions. Nervousness doesn't prevent you from doing the things that God wants us to do. Anxiety, on the other hand, can prevent us from doing God's will and purpose. It makes it difficult to focus and go about our day. Nervousness is a response to something specific, while anxiety is often more general.

It's okay to be a little nervous but keep moving forward knowing God is in control and will guide you. Refrain from being anxious, as it can cause stagnation or standing still. God bless.

What are you nervous/anxious about regarding your business? What can help you believe God is in control to calm your spirit?

_____

_____

_____

_____

_____

_____

_____

44. The Lord's Requests

Good morning entrepreneurs,

And now, Israel, what does the Lord your God ask of you except to fear the Lord your God by walking in all His ways, to love Him, and to worship the Lord your God with all your heart and all your soul? Keep the Lord's commands and statutes I am giving you today, for your own good (Deuteronomy 10:12-13).

COMMENTARY

These are God's instructions to live our lives in a way that is pleasing to Him. It will lead to a peaceful life and a successful business. Challenge yourself for the next 30 days to follow the instructions above and see how your life changes. God bless.

What did God reveal to you through today's devotion?

_____

_____

_____

_____

_____

_____

_____

_____

_____

_____

_____

_____

45. How God Trains Us

Good morning entrepreneurs,
May the Lord, my rock, be praised, who trains my hands for battle and my fingers for warfare (Psalm 144:1).

COMMENTARY

The enemy wants your business to fail so that you will not reach those people that the Lord has for you to help and minister to. We must allow God to train us and fight against those things that keep us from moving forward in our business. Procrastination, fear, naysayers, and lack of confidence are just a few. Praise God each day for training you how to resist what is holding you back. Put on the whole armor of God (Ephesians 6:10-19) and press forward as God guides you in your business! God bless.

What is holding you back? Take time to write an obituary about it here so you can bury it.

_____

_____

_____

_____

_____

_____

_____

_____

_____

46. The Benefits of Wisdom

Good morning entrepreneurs,
Now if any of you lacks wisdom, he should ask God, who gives to all generously and without criticizing, and it will be given to him (James 1:5).

COMMENTARY

What decisions have you made for this year? Have you prayerfully completed your vision board, set your goals and steps, and gone before the Lord with them for His confirmation and wisdom? As godly entrepreneurs, we can no longer "go with our gut" for the decisions of our business and our lives. We must read God's Word daily, then spend time before Him in prayer, listening for direction with pen and paper. If you do not have a daily prayer routine, begin with 10 minutes daily. Dr. Charles Stanley (In Touch Ministries) or a Bible app has excellent daily devotions and reminders to help you establish a daily prayer life. It is essential to your relationship with God, which affects the success of your business and your life. God bless.

What did God reveal to you through today's devotion?

_____

_____

_____

_____

_____

_____

_____

47. Hold onto God's Promises

Good morning entrepreneurs,
Let us hold on to the confession of our hope without wavering, for He who promised is faithful (Hebrews 10:23).

COMMENTARY

Minister Angela Garza, a minister at Friendship Baptist Church of Roslyn, NY said, "Speak the promise not the problem."

Do you share with family and/or friends only the struggles you are facing in your life and business, or do you speak affirmations (positive statements) of God's blessings to you? Don't focus your conversations on the problems but on the truths of God's promises; Isaiah 40:30, Luke 1:37, Mark 9:23, Mark 11:24, and the list goes on. When you are tempted to be discouraged or disappointed about your business, remember, it is in God's hands, and you are merely the steward. Stay focused, be obedient, and have faith. God bless.

What did God reveal to you through today's devotion?

_____

_____

_____

_____

_____

_____

_____

_____

48. Beware of a Stingy Heart

Good morning entrepreneurs,

Give to him, and don't have a stingy heart when you give, and because of this the Lord your God will bless you in all your work and in everything you do (Deuteronomy 15:10).

COMMENTARY

Do you give grudgingly (reluctantly) only because God demands it, or do you give gladly and with a smile? Do you give all that God tells you to or do you hold some back "just to be safe"? Giving and tithing should give us joy because God has blessed us with so much and He only asks for one-tenth. What if He asks for more? Should we do it or do we think we heard incorrectly? God gives so freely to us that it should always fill us with joy to give. If you are reluctant in your giving to God and others, ask God to show you why. God bless.

What did God reveal to you through today's devotion?

_____

_____

_____

_____

_____

_____

_____

_____

_____

49. The Blessings of Being Disciplined

Good morning entrepreneurs,

Therefore, I do not run like one who runs aimlessly or box like one beating the air. Instead, I discipline my body and bring it under strict control, so that after preaching to others, I myself will not be disqualified (1 Corinthians 9:26-27).

COMMENTARY

Nelson's Foundational Bible Dictionary defines discipline as "teaching or training which is designed to strengthen and perfect the character (1 Cor 9:27); systematic training in a certain subject." What are you doing to become more disciplined? Do you begin every day with Bible reading, prayer, and meditation? Do you follow a definite daily routine or schedule? Do you do what you say you will do? Are you faithful to your commitments? Do you seek to stop bad character traits and replace them with godly character traits? A disciplined spiritual life leads to discipline in our business, but we must prayerfully train ourselves to be more disciplined. Here is an excellent article on how self-discipline unlocks God's will for our lives: Marrazzo, Cortni. *"3 Ways Self-Discipline is the Key to Unlocking God's Will."* Crosswalk.Com, August 6, 2020. God bless.

What did God reveal to you through today's devotion?

_____

_____

_____

_____

_____

_____

50. Forgiveness is Healing

Good morning entrepreneurs,
For if you forgive people their wrongdoing, your heavenly Father will forgive you as well. But if you don't forgive people, your (heavenly) Father will not forgive your wrongdoing (Matthew 6:14-15).

COMMENTARY

"I'm sorry." Has anyone hurt you deeply and uttered those words to you, but they sounded hollow? When we are deeply hurt, it just doesn't feel like those words are enough. You want to hurt back; you want them to feel the hurt you feel. But the scripture above says we must forgive, or God will not forgive us. It sounds harsh but that is God's command, and it actually begins our healing process. Unforgiveness cannot only prevent us from hearing God, it can block His blessings for us and cause physical ailments. You cannot undo what someone said or did to you that is hurtful, but you can choose to forgive, prayerfully set your boundaries with that person, and press forward so that God will bless you and your business. God bless.

Identify a past hurt by someone. Write a letter to God asking for help to forgive them.

_____

_____

_____

_____

_____

_____

51. Walk in God's Gift and Good Works

Good morning entrepreneurs,

For you are saved by grace through faith, and this is not from yourselves; it is God's gift—not from works, so that no one can boast. For we are His creation, created in Christ Jesus for good works, which God prepared ahead of time so that we should walk in them (Ephesians 2:8-10).

COMMENTARY

Our business thrives and grows through the gifts God has given us and His purpose and plan for our lives. But how do we learn the plan and our gifts? As we pray for direction in this area, know there are three parts to our life's purpose: sanctification (an ongoing growth in holiness), stewardship (managing our time, talents and spiritual gifts God has blessed us with), and service (inspiring spiritual growth and meeting the physical needs of others and providing encouragement through scripture). It begins with the breaking! As we grow in the above areas of the purpose God has for all believers, our individual purpose and spiritual gifts will be revealed. God has prepared our unique gifts and purpose before we were born. We just need to walk in it as outlined above. We will then see the "Good success" that God told Joshua about. God bless.

What did God reveal to you through today's devotion?

_____

_____

_____

_____

_____

_____

52. How to Be Fruitful

Good morning entrepreneurs,

And our people must also learn to devote themselves to good works for cases of urgent need, so that they will not be unfruitful (Titus 3:14).

COMMENTARY

What does it mean to be fruitful? God has blessed us with a business to produce fruit, the fruit of saving souls and serving through our business. We must be willing to devote some time to our development for this to happen. This means every day you should do something for your business as you are led. When you devote time to your business, you will begin to see the fruit it produces. God bless.

What did God reveal to you through today's devotion?

_____

_____

_____

_____

_____

_____

_____

_____

_____

_____

_____

2nd Phase – Letting Go

We have so much of our old self that we must let go of. Like the blueberry fields in Maine that are burned at the end of the season to stimulate new growth, the Lord breaks and burns our flesh to stimulate growth. After the breaking phase, we should better understand the thoughts, attitudes, and character traits we must let go of for God to use us. As we learn to let go, we must incorporate more fasting into our lives. Fasting teaches us how to deny ourselves and be more obedient to what God is telling us. Denying our fleshly desires and habits is hard, but fasting is a wonderful way to start.

53. Developing the Ministry of Your Business

Good morning entrepreneurs,

But as for you, be serious about everything, endure hardship, do the work of an evangelist, fulfill your ministry (2 Timothy 4:5).

COMMENTARY

Remember your work is to be an evangelist in your business. We work so hard at being successful in the physical aspect of our business that sometimes we let go of the spiritual. It should be the opposite! Every client or customer we encounter is an opportunity to do the work of an evangelist. It doesn't mean you must start quoting scripture. Sometimes it is a smile, a simple compliment, or just listening. Strive to be as successful as an evangelist as you are an entrepreneur! Have a blessed day in the Lord.

What did God reveal to you through today's devotion?

_____

_____

_____

_____

_____

_____

_____

_____

_____

_____

54. Consequences of Wavering Faith

Good morning entrepreneurs,

For we walk by faith, not by sight (2 Corinthians 5:7 HCSB).

COMMENTARY

When we think about Dr. Martin Luther King Jr., most people focus on his speeches and the marches for justice and equality he participated in through a nonviolent approach. Let us also remember he was a man of God who trusted God. He had a dream he never let go of because he had faith God would bring it to fruition, which He did, and it is still ongoing. Likewise, let us not give up on our dreams to have a successful business ministry. "Let us hold on to the confession of our hope without wavering, for He who promised is faithful" (Hebrews 10:23). God bless.

What are your dreams for your business?

_____

_____

_____

_____

_____

_____

_____

_____

_____

55. How Being Silent Can Bless You

Good morning entrepreneurs,
The Lord will fight for you while you [only need to] keep silent and remain calm (Exodus 14:14 AMP).

COMMENTARY

My son pointed this scripture out to me, and it has given me such encouragement. This scripture confirms whatever contrary circumstances we encounter, God will handle it if we keep quiet and remain calm. Then He will fight for us and rectify the situation while the only thing we need to do is to be silent and let go! Sometimes it is easier said than done, but we must have the courage to take God at His Word. God bless.

What did God reveal to you through today's devotion?

_____

_____

_____

_____

_____

_____

_____

_____

_____

_____

56. What God is Telling Me to Do vs. What I Want to Do

Good morning entrepreneurs,

I am able to do all things through Him who strengthens me (Philippians 4:13).

COMMENTARY

The thing you do not want to do is usually the thing God is telling you to do, and He will enable you to do it. If what you are trying to do seems too difficult or is not working out right, either you are doing the wrong thing, or you need to step back and let God take control. He will then give you the strength to complete the task. God bless.

What did God reveal to you through today's devotion?

_____

_____

_____

_____

_____

_____

_____

_____

_____

_____

_____

_____

57.Watching Your Mountains Move Out of Your Way!

Good morning entrepreneurs,

I assure you: If anyone says to this mountain, 'Be lifted up and thrown into the sea,' and does not doubt in his heart, but believes that what he says will happen, it will be done for him (Mark 11:23 HCSB).

COMMENTARY

Pray, in the Name of Jesus (and believe), that God will remove every mountain that is hindering your business from being successful (with no doubt in your mind). Doubt is a seed of the enemy that when planted in our mind, kills our spirit. Do not allow doubt to win. Trust God! God bless.

What must you do to trust God more?

_____

_____

_____

_____

_____

_____

_____

_____

_____

_____

_____

58. More Doors

Good morning entrepreneurs,

I know your works. Because you have limited strength, have kept My word, and have not denied My name, look, I have placed before you an open door that no one is able to close (Revelation 3:8).

COMMENTARY

Your business is an open door that the Lord has blessed you with. Are you walking through it or standing in front of it? Every day is an opportunity to move forward in it. What are you expecting to do today to open the door even wider? God bless.

What did God reveal to you through today's devotion?

_____

_____

_____

_____

_____

_____

_____

_____

_____

_____

_____

_____

59. Gratitude Will Sustain You

Good morning entrepreneurs,

This is the day the Lord has made; let us rejoice and be glad in it (Psalm 118:24).

COMMENTARY

Walk in a spirit of gratitude every day! We so often look at our problems first. Today, ask yourself, "Did I wake up this morning? Am I breathing? Am I reasonably healthy? Do I have a roof over my head? Food to eat and clothes to wear?" Then rejoice in the Lord and have a spirit of gratitude. Our blessings will always outnumber our trials! God bless.

What did God reveal to you through today's devotion?

_____

_____

_____

_____

_____

_____

_____

_____

_____

_____

60. The Joy of Weeping

Good morning entrepreneurs,

For His anger lasts only a moment, but His favor, a lifetime. Weeping may spend the night, but there is joy in the morning (Psalm 30:5).

COMMENTARY

Whatever difficulty you are dealing with in your life that seems like it will never change, remember that a "night" may be years, but God gives you joy in your life every day, just look for it! What is today's joy in your life? God bless.

What did God reveal to you through today's devotion?

_____

_____

_____

_____

_____

_____

_____

_____

_____

_____

_____

_____

_____

61. Follow Your Path

Good morning entrepreneurs,

Let your eyes look forward; fix your gaze straight ahead. Carefully consider the path for your feet, and all your ways will be established (Proverbs 4:25-26).

COMMENTARY

Someone texted me to say she was having difficulty establishing her business plan. She said establishing her business is "hard work." I encouraged her to persevere because her business plan is her roadmap. Business is hard work, but we are blessed to be given this opportunity. As entrepreneurs, we must encourage and support each other. Keep advancing, making tiny or large steps in your business as the Holy Spirit directs. There may be many pitfalls and failures, but each one will give you confidence to face the next one. What pitfalls are you facing? God bless.

What did God reveal to you through today's devotion?

_____

_____

_____

_____

_____

_____

_____

_____

62. Watch Your Time

Good morning entrepreneurs,

Pay careful attention, then, to how you walk—not as unwise people but as wise—making the most of the time, because the days are evil (Ephesians 5:15-16).

COMMENTARY

Do you monitor your time? There are 24 hours in each day. If we give God one-tenth of our time that is 2 hours and 24 minutes each day! We are to pray without ceasing, but we must dedicate specific prayer and meditation time with the Lord. Even if we have a daily schedule, there are hours of wasted time in our day we spend watching television, having idle conversation, mindlessly scrolling through social media, or doing other unproductive things. I'm not saying God doesn't give us free time. What I am saying is we must make the most of our time. This includes scheduling time for the things of God. Once the day is completed, there is no opportunity for a "redo" so make the most of each day! How much time do you spend with God daily? God bless.

What did God reveal to you through today's devotion?

_____

_____

_____

_____

_____

_____

_____

63. A Rock That Lasts Forever

Good morning entrepreneurs,
Trust in the Lord forever, because in Yahweh, the Lord, is an everlasting rock (Isaiah 26:4)!

COMMENTARY

God is our solid rock, and we can always depend on Him. Stones move, but rocks don't move. It takes a backhoe to remove a rock. Sometimes, even with that, they cannot be moved. That is our God. No matter what is going on He knows what we are dealing with, and He is in control. Never think that you are out there by yourself in your business. The One who gave you the idea and the tools to carry it through is with you. What we think is a step backward is really a lesson that we will need going forward. Hold onto God, our everlasting rock. God bless.

How do you know God is your rock?

_____

_____

_____

_____

_____

_____

_____

_____

_____

64. Prepare to Endure

Good morning entrepreneurs,

See, we count as blessed those who have endured. You have heard of Job's endurance and have seen the outcome from the Lord. The Lord is very compassionate and merciful (James 5:11).

COMMENTARY

Don't give up on growing your business. The idea God has given you is unique to you, that is why you must grow in your relationship with the Lord so He can guide you. Well-meaning people will give you advice, but it won't work for you. Only the people God sends to you can give you advice. Over time you will know the difference. Continue to endure and persevere. What do you do to endure in your business? God bless.

What did God reveal to you through today's devotion?

_____

_____

_____

_____

_____

_____

_____

_____

_____

_____

65. How to Gain Confidence

Good morning entrepreneurs,
For the Lord will be your confidence and will keep your foot from a snare
(Proverbs 3:26).

COMMENTARY

Don't be afraid of failures or mistakes. Without setbacks, we won't learn. Without failures, we won't have a desire to seek the Lord more and more. Be confident that whatever mistakes or failures you make, God is with you, and it is an opportunity to grow stronger and wiser in what He wants you to accomplish. What do you do when you make a mistake? God bless.

What did God reveal to you through today's devotion?

_____

_____

_____

_____

_____

_____

_____

_____

_____

_____

_____

_____

66. What is the Real Vision for Your Business?

Good morning entrepreneurs,

The Lord answered me: "Write down this vision; clearly inscribe it on tablets so, one may easily read it. For the vision is yet for the appointed time; it testifies about the end and will not lie. Though it delays, wait for it, since it will certainly come and not be late" (Habakkuk 2:2-3).

COMMENTARY

What vision has God given you for your business? Write it down so that you can see it. Then make the first step the Holy Spirit gives you, then the second step and so on. You can't go to step two until you have completed step one. Take each step as the Lord instructs. Then watch as God brings it to fruition. God bless.

What did God reveal to you through today's devotion?

_____

_____

_____

_____

_____

_____

_____

_____

_____

_____

_____

67. The Crippling Effect of Fear

Good morning entrepreneurs,
For God has not given us a spirit of fearfulness, but one of power, love, and sound judgment (2 Timothy 1:7).

Are you fearful of moving forward with your business? Do you have a fear that if it is successful, you won't be able to manage it? Or is it fear of failure? Fear of ridicule/criticism? Why do we focus on the fear but not the power, love, and sound judgement of Jesus? Take time to reflect on the fears you have regarding your business and give them to Jesus to move forward with God's plan. Face your fears then let go of them. They will disappear when you truly trust God! What is your biggest fear for your business? Have a productive and blessed day.

What did God reveal to you through today's devotion?

_____

_____

_____

_____

_____

_____

_____

_____

_____

_____

68. There is Success in Waiting on God

Good morning entrepreneurs,

Now, Lord, what do I wait for? My hope is in You (Psalm 39:7).

COMMENTARY

Have you become stagnant in your business? If you have, is it because you're waiting on God to tell you when to move or are you just waiting (procrastinating, fearful, unsure)? Waiting on God is an active exercise not passive. Spend time with the Lord today and ask Him, "Lord, what is the next step for my business?" Then go do it! What are you waiting for? God bless.

What did God reveal to you through today's devotion?

---

69. A Reason to Rise Early

Good morning entrepreneurs,
At daybreak, Lord, you hear my voice; at daybreak I plead my case to You and watch expectantly (Psalm 5:3).

COMMENTARY

Why does each devotion begin with "Good morning?" What time do you get up to pray? Perhaps you do it on the run or at the end of the day. There is something about getting up early in the morning to spend time with God. Perhaps you are not an early riser, but God is! I can tell you that I did not become an early riser until I had children. Then, as I desired to have a closer relationship with God, I would ask God when I prayed at night to wake me up early enough to spend time with Him. He absolutely did that. At 3 or 4 am, He would wake me up, and after lying in bed for 15-20 minutes, I would realize He was not letting me go back to sleep. It is such a blessing to spend time with the Lord before the world gets up and things get noisy and hectic. Give it a try to see how God blesses you. Pray, expecting God to answer your prayers. God bless.

What did God reveal to you through today's devotion?

_____

_____

_____

_____

_____

_____

70. Are You Consistent?

Good morning entrepreneurs,
Read Daniel 6:1-28.

COMMENTARY

"The Power of Genuine Consistency" is real! Our morals, character, behavior, principles, and daily routine should be consistent. Family should know that we are praying each morning; co-workers and friends should know God comes first in our lives and see His Spirit shining through us (Matthew 5:16). Even those who don't know should see God's light shining through us. Please take some time to read this scripture today, and allow Daniel's consistency to inspire you to become more consistent in all that you do. God bless.

How consistent are you and where do you need to improve?

_____

_____

_____

_____

_____

_____

_____

_____

_____

_____

71. No Goals, No Results

Good morning entrepreneurs,

Therefore, I do not run without a definite goal; I do not flail around like one beating the air [just shadow boxing]. But [like a boxer] I strictly discipline my body and make it my slave, so that, after I have preached [the gospel] to others, I myself will not somehow be disqualified [as unfit for service] (1 Corinthians 9:26-27 AMP).

COMMENTARY

If we are to be successful entrepreneurs, we must have goals. How can we minister to others and share the importance of having goals if we do not have them? Our first goal must be creating our business plan, guided by the Holy Spirit. This seems like a repetitious devotion, and it is! It is because you must have a business plan to be successful. If you have difficulty, contact the Small Business Administration (www.score.org) to find a mentor or attend a free workshop. No business is successful without a plan! God bless.

What did God reveal to you through today's devotion?

_____

_____

_____

_____

_____

_____

_____

72. The Magnificence of Yahweh

Good morning entrepreneurs,
Yahweh, our Lord, how magnificent is Your Name throughout the earth (Psalm 8:1 AMP)!

COMMENTARY

Do we understand how amazing our God is? Do we know that He is King of kings? Do we believe that He can do all things? If we know these things, then we must believe that He will do what He says! He says that we are His workmanship and He created us for good works. Our business is His good work, and we must believe that God will move us to levels we never dreamed of, if we only believe that He is all powerful. Do you believe it? God bless.

What did God reveal to you through today's devotion?

_____

_____

_____

_____

_____

_____

_____

_____

_____

_____

73. Desires and Motivation

Good morning entrepreneurs,

You desire and do not have. You murder and covet and cannot obtain. You fight and war. You do not have because you do not ask. You ask and don't receive because you ask with wrong motives, so that you may spend it on your evil desires (James 4:2-3).

COMMENTARY

Have you asked God for something but have not received it? Check you motives (reason) for asking. If you ask with the wrong motives (selfish, manipulative, or for self-gain), those prayers will not be answered. It is usually not what we ask God, it is because our motives are wrong. What are your motives for the prayers you have asked God to answer? God bless.

What did God reveal to you through today's devotion?

_____

_____

_____

_____

_____

_____

_____

_____

_____

_____

74. Who Are Your Mentors?

Good morning entrepreneurs,
Therefore, since we also have such a large cloud of witnesses surrounding us, let us lay aside every weight and the sin that so easily ensnares us. Let us run with endurance the race that lies before us (Hebrews 12:1).

COMMENTARY

All athletes have a coach. Someone who will encourage, support, and push them when they want to give up. Someone who has wisdom in the sport they are playing and can give them information based on their experiences to make the athlete better. As an entrepreneur, we need mentors. Someone who will cheer us on, but also let us know when we are going astray. Don't give up or give in. God has blessed us with a calling, a race to run. Don't give up. Ask God to send a mentor to help you. God bless.

What did God reveal to you through today's devotion?

_____

_____

_____

_____

_____

_____

_____

_____

_____

75. Planning and Working

Good morning entrepreneurs,

For we are His creation, created in Christ Jesus for good works, which God prepared ahead of time so that we should walk in them (Ephesians 2:10).

Today's devotion is a simple prayer: Father, help us to walk in the plan you created for me. God bless.

What did God reveal to you through today's devotion?

_____

_____

_____

_____

_____

_____

_____

_____

_____

_____

_____

_____

_____

_____

76. Where is Your Focus?

Good morning entrepreneurs,

You will keep in perfect and constant peace the one whose mind is steadfast [that is, committed and focused on You—in both inclination and character], Because he trusts and takes refuge in You [with hope and confident expectation] (Isaiah 26:3 AMP).

COMMENTARY

Are you frazzled or confused about your business? Sometimes we lose our focus. When we lose our focus, we can lose our peace. If God is the creator of your business and you keep your focus on Him, you won't be worried about your business. God will guide and instruct you every day and every step of the way. When you find yourself becoming worried about your business or life in general, ask God to help you focus on Him. God bless.

What are you worried about and why?

_____

_____

_____

_____

_____

_____

_____

_____

_____

77. Making a Vow to the Lord for Your Business

Good morning entrepreneurs,

When a man makes a vow to the Lord or swears an oath to put himself under an obligation, he must not break his word; he must do whatever he has promised (Numbers 30:2).

Have you promised the Lord that you would commit to establishing the business He has called you to? If yes, you must take every opportunity that God sends to you. He will put people and learning opportunities in your path to teach you how to manage your business in excellence. Remember God assigned you to establish this business so that you can minister to those He sends to you. The business belongs to God, we are the managers/stewards. What are you doing to grow in your management skills? God bless.

What did God reveal to you through today's devotion?

_____

_____

_____

_____

_____

_____

_____

_____

_____

_____

78. Have a Network of Connectors

Good morning entrepreneurs,

So then, we must pursue what promotes peace and what builds up one another (Romans 14:19).

COMMENTARY

I was asked to speak at an event at an African American museum. As part of the event, a professional photographer took a photo of each of the speakers for their professional use. The photographer and I connected that day and have stayed in touch. One day, she came to my house to update my professional photos, as I requested it. It was a beautiful experience, and the cost was acceptable for me. Oh yes, and as we spoke, I learned she is a Christian. I met another lady who is now my publisher for this book. I share this because:

1. You should always be open to meeting new people as you never know who God is sending to help you, or you can help them. We must support, encourage, and build up each other in this service of entrepreneurship.

2. As entrepreneurs, you should consider having a professional photo done. This way when God sends an event or opportunity your way and they ask for a photo, you will be ready! God bless.

What did God reveal to you through today's devotion?

_____

_____

_____

_____

_____

79. Giving Birth to Your Business

Good morning entrepreneurs,

Then the angel told her: Do not be afraid, Mary, for you have found favor with God. Now listen: You will conceive and give birth to a son, and you will call His name Jesus (Luke 1:30-31).

COMMENTARY

Elder Audrey Lewis, Friendship Baptist Church, Roslyn, New York, preached a sermon titled "Bring Forth". In the sermon, she talked about how God makes the useless useful. She said there are three requirements to bring forth the gift God has deposited in us: first, we must be willing to be uncomfortable; second, we must be willing to travail (toil); and third, we must be willing to abide in Christ. To give birth to our business is like giving birth to a child. It is not easy, but the joy it brings is unspeakable. Are you feeling uncomfortable about your business? Now it is time to step out and "Bring Forth!" God bless.

What did God reveal to you through today's devotion?

_____

_____

_____

_____

_____

_____

_____

_____

80. The Impossible Becoming Possible

Good morning entrepreneurs,

And looking at them, Jesus said to them, "With people this is impossible, but with God all things are possible] (Matthew 19:26 NASB).

COMMENTARY

When you think about your business today, don't be discouraged and don't let it overwhelm you. All things are possible with God, and, as the quote by Nelson Mandela implies, "It looks impossible until it is done." That's because we are looking at this assignment through our eyes and not God's. Visualize what you want your business to look like. What do you want it to say about you? What is your branding? Who can help you develop it? Let the impossible become possible as you look through God's eyes! God bless.

What did God reveal to you through today's devotion?

_____

_____

_____

_____

_____

_____

_____

_____

_____

_____

81. Accept God's Help

Good morning entrepreneurs,
For I, Yahweh your God, hold your right hand and say to you: Do not fear,
I will help you (Isaiah 41:13).

COMMENTARY

Hold tight to God's hand, let go of your fear, and quickly move to the next level of your business ministry that God has shown you. Keep moving. Keep going, don't stop, and don't let anything scare you. You all know the voice of the Holy Spirit; listen and do what you hear the Spirit telling you! Isaiah 43:2 says, "I will be with you when you pass through the waters, and when you pass through the rivers, they will not overwhelm you. You will not be scorched when you walk through the fire, and the flame will not burn you."

Don't fear making the wrong choice. Every step will be a victory or a lesson! God's got you; keep moving forward! God bless.

What did God reveal to you through today's devotion?

_____

_____

_____

_____

_____

_____

_____

_____

82. Look Back but Don't Stay There!

Good morning entrepreneurs,
Brothers and sisters, I do not consider that I have made it my own yet; but one thing I do: forgetting what lies behind and reaching forward to what lies ahead, I press on toward the goal to win the [heavenly] prize of the upward call of God in Christ Jesus (Philippians 3:14-15 AMP).

COMMENTARY

"The past is a place of reference, not a place of residence; the past is a place of learning, not a place of living." — Roy T. Bennett

Why do you look back? Do you live in the past or the present? If we are to let go of the old person, we cannot continue to look back. By doing so, we are focusing more on the past than the future. Look back only to learn, be in the present and follow God's direction, and press forward into the future and plans God has for you! God bless.

What did God reveal to you through today's devotion?

_____

_____

_____

_____

_____

_____

_____

_____

_____

83. A Foundation of Strength

Good morning entrepreneurs,

But the Lord is faithful, and He will strengthen you [setting you on a firm foundation] and will protect and guard you from the evil one (2 Thessalonians 3:3 AMP).

COMMENTARY

As we grow stronger in the Lord and share His Word with more and more people, we must remember to ask God for His protection daily. The enemy is waiting for any opportunity to distract or harm us, BUT God will protect us and gives us the Holy Spirit to guide us. Be on your guard daily and put on the *whole armor of God* (Ephesians 6:10-18). God bless.

What did God reveal to you through today's devotion?

_____

_____

_____

_____

_____

_____

_____

_____

_____

84. The Blessings of a True Friend

Good morning entrepreneurs,

A friend loves at all times, and a brother is born for a difficult time (Proverbs 17:17 HCSB).

COMMENTARY

You won't know who your true friends or true brothers and sisters are until you are in dire need of something or experiencing difficult times. They are there when you need them, ready and willing to help and comfort. True friends are like gold and are few in number. Do you have a godly friend like that? Even more important, are you that kind of godly friend? God bless.

What did God reveal to you through today's devotion?

_____

_____

_____

_____

_____

_____

_____

_____

_____

_____

_____

_____

85. The Basis of Your Confidence

Good morning entrepreneurs,

The man who trusts in the Lord, whose confidence indeed is the Lord, is blessed (Jeremiah 17:7).

COMMENTARY

I like to refer to my confidence, not as self-confidence, but godly confidence. We step out, trusting in God, following His instruction and direction, and He will empower us. It is His power that gives us confidence to do things we would not do or be hesitant to do on our own. What kind of confidence do you have? God bless.

What did God reveal to you through today's devotion?

_____

_____

_____

_____

_____

_____

_____

_____

_____

_____

_____

_____

86. The Lord is With You

Good morning entrepreneurs,

But I tell you the truth, it is to your advantage that I go away; for if I do not go away, the Helper (Comforter, Advocate, Intercessor—Counselor, Strengthener, Standby) will not come to you; but if I go, I will send Him (the Holy Spirit) to you [to be in close fellowship with you] (John 16:7 AMP).

COMMENTARY

As God leads you to do new things, as your territory and ministry grow, you may feel uncertainty and uncomfortable. God promises to be with us to provide what we need and to guide us. Move in the vision God has given you. Why do you hesitate? God bless.

What did God reveal to you through today's devotion?

_____

_____

_____

_____

_____

_____

_____

_____

_____

_____

_____

87. Stay on Point with Your Plan

Good morning entrepreneurs,
The plans of the diligent certainly lead to profit, but anyone who is reckless certainly becomes poor (Proverbs 21:5).

COMMENTARY

Are you following your business plan? Your business plan is your blueprint for your business. Without a plan, you have no strategy and are building your business carelessly.

Read the above scripture again and refer to the previous devotions on business plans. Are you drafting your blueprint? God bless.

What did God reveal to you through today's devotion?

_____

_____

_____

_____

_____

_____

_____

_____

_____

_____

_____

_____

88. Denying Yourself for the Journey

Good morning entrepreneurs,

"Even now," says the Lord, "Turn and come to Me with all your heart [in genuine repentance], With fasting and weeping and mourning until every barrier is removed, and the broken fellowship is restored" (Joel 2:12 AMP).

COMMENTARY

Let your fasting not just be a time of giving up some things (sweets, television, etc.) and doing other things (serving more, praying more, etc.). Let it also be a time in which you draw closer to God and into a stronger, deeper relationship with Him. Let fasting not be about what you give up, but what you gain! If you never fasted before, read the following, (Luke 5:33-35, Galatians 5:16, Matthew 6:16-18, Daniel 9:2-5). Also, here is an article that may help: Mathis, David. "A Guide to Christian Fasting." Desiring God, May 4, 2023. Fasting can change your life! God bless.

What did God reveal to you through today's devotion?

89. Does My Business Reflect Christ?

Good morning entrepreneurs,

I have been crucified with Christ [that is, in Him I have shared His crucifixion]; it is no longer I who live, but Christ lives in me. The life I now live in the body I live by faith [by adhering to, relying on, and completely trusting] in the Son of God, who loved me and gave Himself up for me (Galatians 2:20).

COMMENTARY

The more we surrender ourselves and are obedient to do what God called us to do, the more we see the Holy Spirit work through us to accomplish God's work. We know it is God doing these things, because there is no way that we could have done it on our own or even wanted to do it! But it is the obedience that pushes us. Each assignment we complete for the Lord leads to the next one. Thank You Jesus for teaching us to walk in the obedience of the Lord. What more do you need to surrender? God bless.

What did God reveal to you through today's devotion?

_____

_____

_____

_____

_____

_____

_____

_____

90. Every Day is a New Start

Good morning entrepreneurs,

It is because of the Lord's lovingkindness that we are not consumed, because His tender compassions never fail. They are new every morning; great and beyond measure is your faithfulness. (Lamentations 3:22-24)

COMMENTARY

In this phase of breaking, how do we begin to start anew? We must ask God to help us do a 180 degree turn in our lives. Everything that we thought to be correct, whether from our parents' teaching to our own experiences, must be examined before God. He gives us mercy and compassion each day so that we can confess our sins, turn from our own ways, and follow His instructions. Let's accept God's faithfulness and begin to make the journey toward the new person God wants us to be!

What is the first thing you must ask God to help you turn away from as you begin your journey of newness?

_____

_____

_____

_____

_____

_____

_____

_____

_____

91. When You Get Weary

Good morning entrepreneurs,
For I (fully) satisfy the weary soul and I replenish every languishing and sorrowful person (Jeremiah 31:25).

COMMENTARY

Sometimes we get weary. We are overworked or things just don't seem to be progressing. The scripture above says we must allow God to saturate our soul when weary and replenish us for the journey. We replenish by spending time with God, resting, and spending time with family. How do you replenish when you get weary? God bless.

What did God reveal to you through today's devotion?

_____

_____

_____

_____

_____

_____

_____

_____

_____

_____

_____

92. Be Careful Who You Walk With

Good morning entrepreneurs,

Blessed [fortunate, prosperous, and favored by God] is the man who does not walk in the counsel of the wicked [following their advice and example], Nor stand in the path of sinners, nor sit [down to rest] in the seat of scoffers [ridiculers] (Psalm 1:1 AMP)

COMMENTARY

Be careful who you listen to, who you associate with and who you allow to guide you in your business. If you prayerfully choose counsel for your business, you will discover that God connects you with wise, godly people. You can't share details of your business with everyone. Sometimes you will share with someone who does not have your best interest in mind. When you discover this, do not continue to confide in that person. Wise counsel is sent by God. Who do you walk and share with? God bless.

What did God reveal to you through today's devotion?

_____

_____

_____

_____

_____

_____

_____

_____

93. Follow the Rules

Good morning entrepreneurs,

This Book of the Law shall not depart from your mouth, but you shall read [and meditate on] it day and night, so that you may be careful to do [everything] in accordance with all that is written in it; for then you will make your way prosperous, and then you will be successful (Joshua 1:8 AMP).

COMMENTARY

How can we do EVERYTHING that is written in the Bible? Matthew Henry Commentary on the Bible explains it this way: "Concerning this book, he {Joshua} is charged, [1.] To meditate therein day and night, that he might understand it and have it ready in him upon all occasions. Those that make the Word of God their rule, and conscientiously walk by that rule, shall both do well and speed {move quickly} well" (Henry, Matthew. 1706. Matthew Henry Commentary on the Whole Bible {Complete}. January 7, 2022). Our business will become successful when we learn (and remember) the Word of God and conscientiously (intentionally, habitually) walk in and live by the Word daily. God bless.

What did God reveal to you through today's devotion?

_____

_____

_____

_____

_____

94. Repetition is Good

Good morning entrepreneurs,

Therefore, I will always be ready to remind you of these things, even though you already know them and are established in the truth which is held firmly in your grasp (2 Peter 1:12 AMP).

COMMENTARY

When someone shares a truth or information you think you already know, don't be so quick to brush them off by saying, "I know that." Instead, listen. The Lord may be leading them to add new information that you didn't know. Or perhaps you are being told something you know but need to be reminded of. As you read these devotions, you may find what you believe is repetition. James 1:19 (AMP) says, "Be quick to listen and slow to speak." Help us, Lord, to listen more, speak less, and not be annoyed by wise words that seem repetitious. God bless.

What did God reveal to you through today's devotion?

_____

_____

_____

_____

_____

_____

_____

_____

95. Thank You Lord for the Failures

Good morning entrepreneurs,
When he falls, he will not be hurled down, Because the Lord is the One who holds his hand and sustains him (Psalm 37:24 AMP).

COMMENTARY

Donnie McClurkin sings a song entitled "We Fall Down" (but we get up). Failures are lessons to be learned, not opportunities to give up. When we fail at a task or idea, stay down long enough to say, "Lord, what are you trying to show me in this failure?" Then get up, with wisdom gained from the failure, and keep moving. Don't wallow in your failures. God loves us and wants to bless us with the desires of our heart. Think of how you bless your children, grandchildren, nieces, and nephews, even when they fail. God is love and His love for us is perfect compared to our love for others. Ask God to bless your business, breathe on it, and mold it according to His plan. Then watch your business grow like never before! God bless.

What setbacks have you had in your business and what lessons did God teach you?

_____

_____

_____

_____

_____

_____

_____

96. Holding on to Wisdom and Instruction

Good morning entrepreneurs,

The [reverent] fear of the Lord [that is, worshiping Him and regarding Him as truly awesome] is the beginning and the preeminent part of knowledge [its starting point and its essence]. But arrogant fools despise [skillful and godly] wisdom and instruction and self-discipline (Proverbs 1:7 AMP).

COMMENTARY

We must gain wisdom to be successful entrepreneurs, but how do we attain wisdom? The scripture above says we must first have knowledge, which begins with reverent fear of the Lord. Next, we must be willing to take instruction, learn skills, and have self-discipline to apply what we learn. There are so many ways to gain knowledge and skills these days! Webinars, podcasts, workshops (which may all be free), and conferences are just a few. Scripture says only a fool despises wisdom and instruction. We must become excited to learn all that we can about our product or service, knowing that God will transform it into wisdom to help others and fulfill our purpose. God bless.

What did God reveal to you through today's devotion?

_____

_____

_____

_____

_____

_____

_____

97. Our Decision - Do What is Good or What the Lord Requires

Good morning entrepreneurs,

He has told you, O man, what is good; And what does the LORD *require of you except to be just, and to love [and to diligently practice] kindness (compassion), and to walk humbly with your God [setting aside any overblown sense of importance or self-righteousness]* (Micah 6:8)?

COMMENTARY

The beginning of the scripture says, "He has told you, o man, what is good and what does the Lord require of you." Wow! According to this scripture, the Lord commands us to do both. We must do what He requires (His commandments) and what is good (to serve and help others as He leads). These characteristics are not complicated, but we need the Lord's help to do them consistently. Let us remember each day how the Lord requires us to live. Think about it. Where are you lacking when it comes to doing what the Lord requires and what is good? God bless.

What did God reveal to you through today's devotion?

_____

_____

_____

_____

_____

_____

_____

98. The Importance of Supporting One Another

Good morning entrepreneurs,

Two are better than one because they have a more satisfying return for their labor; for if either of them falls, the one will lift up his companion. But woe to him who is alone when he falls and does not have another to lift him up (Eccl. 4:9-10 AMP).

COMMENTARY

As we build our business, we need godly people around us to support, encourage and give us wise counsel. We in turn need to do this for someone else. Notice how God connects us with other godly people. He doesn't want us to walk alone as we deal with the issues of our business. When we encounter difficult situations, be on the lookout; God is sending help. God bless.

What did God reveal to you through today's devotion?

_____

_____

_____

_____

_____

_____

_____

_____

_____

_____

99. Know What Concerns You

Good morning entrepreneurs,

The Lord will accomplish that which concerns me. Your [unwavering] lovingkindness, O Lord, endures forever—Do not abandon the works of Your own hands (Psalm 138:8 AMP).

COMMENTARY

Godly entrepreneurs are following the Lord's calling to establish a business. We are concerned that it will be successful, that we are hearing the Lord correctly, and that it will be a blessing to others. The scripture above says the Lord will accomplish (bring to conclusion or finish) the things that trouble or worry us. Ask God to lead you, then wait for His direction as He prepares you to move in the right direction for success. Have you shared with the Lord what is worrying you today? God bless.

What did God reveal to you through today's devotion?

_____

_____

_____

_____

_____

_____

_____

_____

_____

100. Defining Patient Endurance

Good morning entrepreneurs,

For you have need of patient endurance [to bear up under difficult circumstances without compromising], so that when you have carried out the will of God, you may receive and enjoy to the full what is promised (Hebrews 10:36 AMP).

COMMENTARY

Don't be discouraged, procrastinate, give up, or slow down. No matter how tired you get, press forward, standing on the promises of God. Keep moving forward in the name of Jesus to fulfill and enjoy what God has promised you. God bless.

What did God reveal to you through today's devotion?

_____

_____

_____

_____

_____

_____

_____

_____

_____

_____

_____

101. Be Careful Not to Stumble

Good morning entrepreneurs,

Therefore see that you walk carefully [living life with honor, purpose, and courage; shunning those who tolerate and enable evil], not as the unwise, but as wise [sensible, intelligent, discerning people], making the very most of your time [on earth, recognizing and taking advantage of each opportunity and using it with wisdom and diligence], because the days are [filled with] evil. (Ephesians 5:15-16 AMP).

COMMENTARY

Time is precious. God has blessed each of us with a measure of time. We don't know how many years it will be, but He gave us the free will to decide how to use it. When we are young, we don't worry about time because we think we have all the time in the world. As we age, we realize the truth in the scripture above to make the most of our time and opportunities. Be careful to take every opportunity that God sends to you. How do you spend your time? God bless.

What did God reveal to you through today's devotion?

_____

_____

_____

_____

_____

_____

_____

_____

102. Give God Your Heart

Good morning entrepreneurs,

And he said to him, "You shall love the Lord your God with all your heart and with all your soul and with all your mind" (Matthew 22:37).

COMMENTARY

Seeking God with your whole heart (not half-heartedly) means letting go of your past, your hurts, your sins, and putting all your thoughts and focus on hearing God. When you do this sincerely, you will begin to hear Him more clearly than ever before. I challenge you to take this day, ask God to help you put aside distracting thoughts so you can concentrate on hearing from Him. During your busy day, can you hear God speaking to you? How do you respond? God bless.

What did God reveal to you through today's devotion?

_____

_____

_____

_____

_____

_____

_____

_____

_____

_____

103. Don't Let the Naysayers Discourage You

Good morning entrepreneurs,

Fret not yourself because of evildoers, neither be envious against those who work unrighteousness (that which is not upright or in right standing with God).For they shall soon be cut down like the grass, and wither as the green herb.Trust (lean on, rely on, and be confident) in the Lord and do good; so, shall you dwell in the land and feed surely on His faithfulness, and truly you shall be fed (Psalm 37:1-3).

COMMENTARY

Whether it is a family member, friend, or co-worker, do not allow those outside of your godly sphere of influence to discourage you. They do not understand that you do not follow the path that worldly entrepreneurs follow. You follow the path God gives you. You may not see the path, but you see a direction and you believe God. People may call you short-sighted, foolish, or even crazy. But they obviously don't know the God you know. Don't allow them to deter you from your path! God bless.

What did God reveal to you through today's devotion?

_____

_____

_____

_____

_____

_____

104. Refrain from Procrastination

Good morning entrepreneurs,

The soul (appetite) of the lazy person craves and gets nothing [for lethargy overcomes ambition], But the soul (appetite) of the diligent [who works willingly] is rich and abundantly supplied (Proverbs 13:4 AMP).

COMMENTARY

Starting a business requires diligent (constant) efforts to be successful. This means, first, receiving confirmation from God that this is His will and plan for you. Please take time to pray, fast, and ask God to confirm this is the season for your business. You are almost one-half of the way through this devotional. Assess where you are and what God has brought you through. Don't give up, keep pressing! God bless.

What did God reveal to you through today's devotion?

_____

_____

_____

_____

_____

_____

_____

_____

_____

_____

105. Do Your Best for Your Business

Good morning entrepreneurs,

Whatever you do [whatever your task may be], work from the soul [that is, put in your very best effort], as [something done] for the Lord and not for men (Colossians 3:23-24 MSG).

COMMENTARY

As godly men and women, we must put our very best effort into everything we do because we are God's ambassadors. People are watching us to see how we behave and how God is working in our lives. Work steadily on your business, a little each day, giving it your best effort for the Lord. What does your best effort look like? God bless.

What did God reveal to you through today's devotion?

_____

_____

_____

_____

_____

_____

_____

_____

_____

_____

106. Are Your Plans in Line with God's Plan?

Good morning entrepreneurs,

A man's mind plans his way [as he journeys through life], But the Lord directs his steps and establishes them (Proverbs 16:9 AMP).

COMMENTARY

If you are to be successful, you MUST follow God's direction. Only He knows the true plan for success. We can make what we believe are the right plans, but make sure to take them before the Lord for His approval. What is the Lord saying to you about your business? God bless.

What did God reveal to you through today's devotion?

_____

_____

_____

_____

_____

_____

_____

_____

_____

_____

_____

107. The Benefits of Godly Mentors

Good morning entrepreneurs,
Without consultation and wise advice, plans are frustrated, but with many counselors they are established and succeed (Proverbs 15:22 AMP).

COMMENTARY

When starting my business, I realized there was so much I didn't know. One of the greatest blessings was the godly mentors who helped me. They saw something in me I didn't see in myself, and I was willing to let them teach me. Some were Christians and some were not. Some were with me for a season, and some are still with me. Years ago, I went to get my hair done at a salon and spa someone recommended. The stylist introduced me to the owner and told her I was an etiquette consultant. The owner asked me about doing a workshop for her staff. Then she said, "You must improve your image" and she helped me to do that. I didn't get offended because she was the expert in her field and was reaching out to help a stranger. Someone else helped me to create my logo and branding which, I knew nothing about.

Ask God to send people into your life who are wiser than you and will give you guidance in all aspects of your business. Then, be willing to prayerfully take their advice. How do you react when someone shares advice about your business? God bless.

What did God reveal to you through today's devotion?

_____

_____

_____

_____

108. Overflowing Confidence

Good morning entrepreneurs,
Blessed [with spiritual security] is the man who believes and trusts in and relies on the Lord And whose hope and confident expectation is the Lord (Jeremiah 17:7 AMP).

COMMENTARY

Our confidence must be built on God. We expect, therefore, if I prepare as God has shown me, He will stand with me. If you don't like to speak in public, ask God to give you the confidence to speak the words He gives you about your business. If you are not an organized person, ask the Lord to show you how to become organized. Every step in our day should begin with a prayer that asks God to give us the confidence we need for the day. We lack confidence because of past failures, negative comments, and lack of self-worth. We must give that all to God and trust Him to be our confidence. If God has called us to do something, He will equip us to do it. We need not be fearful of failing or being embarrassed because God is right there speaking to us and guiding us. Our part is to be obedient. Move in your business with godly confidence. Philippians 4:13 says, "I can do all things through Jesus Christ who strengthens me." Matthew 19:26 says, "There is nothing impossible with God." Romans 8:31 says, "If God is for you, who can be against you?" These are confidence scriptures to encourage you as you operate your business. Memorize them, believe them, and stand on them! God bless.

What did God reveal to you through today's devotion?

_____

_____

_____

_____

_____

_____

_____

_____

_____

_____

_____

_____

_____

_____

_____

_____

_____

_____

3rd Phase – Planting and Cultivating

After you break ground, you must cultivate it. That means you must prepare the soil for raising new crops. In spiritual terms, it means, after God has broken us, He raises us up to be the purposeful servants He created us to be. There is still work to be done in us, but we are now receptive to receive the changes God wants to make in us. This phase focuses on nurturing the "new you" after the letting go of the old you. As God's entrepreneur, your branding reflects who you are. As God cultivates your new character, pray about your branding for your business. This is a part of the planting and cultivating.

109. Be a Good Decision Maker

Good morning entrepreneurs,

Let this mind be in you, which was also in Christ Jesus (Philippians 2:5 KJV).

COMMENTARY

Decisions, decisions, decisions! So many decisions for an entrepreneur to make. Every day we must make crucial decisions that will affect our business and our personal lives; finances, location, products, marketing, staff, clients, and the list goes on. The good news is that we have the mind of Christ and all the answers we need to be successful. The bad news is we don't always listen, and we don't always wait for His response.

Here are several more scriptures to consider in our decision-making process:

Proverbs 3:5-6, Philippians 4:6-7 (if you are anxious about a decision, that is when we must wait), James 1:5 (ask God for wisdom daily), Isaiah 30:21, Proverbs 18:5. You may add to this list, "The characteristics of an entrepreneur: motivation, passion, vision, confidence, decision-making (Nick Rojas, *5 Characteristics of an Entrepreneur).* Interestingly, the Holy Spirit led me to scriptural principles to confirm these basic characteristics of a godly entrepreneur as well. God bless.

What did God reveal to you through today's devotion?

_____

_____

_____

110. The Learning Process

Good morning entrepreneurs,

And now, Israel, what does the Lord your God require from you, but to fear [and worship] the Lord your God [with awe-filled reverence and profound respect], to walk [that is, to live each and every day] in all His ways and to love Him, and to serve the Lord your God with all your heart and with all your soul [your choices, your thoughts, your whole being], and to keep the commandments of the Lord and His statutes which I am commanding you today for your good (Deut. 10:12-13 AMP).

COMMENTARY

"Obedience is a learning process" is a favorite saying of mine. As we make goals, we must remember that our ultimate goal must be to obey God and that His commands are for our good. As we are being cultivated, it is an ongoing act of growth and development to be practiced daily. We must: 1. Fear and worship God; 2. Walk every day in His way; 3. Love Him; 4. Serve Him with ALL my heart and soul, my choices, and thoughts; and 5. Keep His commandments. Doing these five things throughout each day helps us to hear from God more clearly and walk in a state of obedience. What thing do you need to ask God to help you with the most? God bless.

What did God reveal to you through today's devotion?

_____

_____

_____

_____

_____

_____

111. Speak the Vision!

Good morning entrepreneurs,

One night the Lord said to Paul in a vision, "Do not be afraid anymore, but go on speaking and do not be silent; for I am with you, and no one will attack you in order to hurt you, because I have many people in this city (Acts 18:9-10).

COMMENTARY

The words God speaks to you in that still, small voice are for direction and to make His vision clear to you. Always be ready to speak when you are urged by the Holy Spirit. Even if it is a powerful or intimidating person, God will protect and guard you just as He did for Paul. He may be using you to bless that person and to provide a need for your business. Also, always be ready to speak out to tell others how you have this business when asked. I share this information out of my personal journey as a shy person. It is a blessing of the Lord. God bless.

What did God reveal to you through today's devotion?

_____

_____

_____

_____

_____

_____

_____

_____

112. The Power of God's Authority

Good morning entrepreneurs,
I sought the Lord [on the authority of His word], and He answered me, and delivered me from all my fears (Psalm 34:4 AMP).

COMMENTARY

Fear. It is an emotion that I have mentioned several times. It is one of the greatest tricks of the enemy to keep us from doing what God has called us to do. As we are planting, we must step out on faith, be obedient to God's voice, and take those steps out of the boat to do "a new thing."

Ralph Waldo Emerson, lecture and philosopher said, "He who is not every day conquering some fear has not learned the secret of life." What fear have these devotions and time spent with God helped you to overcome? God bless.

What did God reveal to you through today's devotion?

_____

_____

_____

_____

_____

_____

_____

_____

113. The Consequences of Presuming

Good morning entrepreneurs,

Through pride and presumption come nothing but strife, but [skillful and godly] wisdom is with those who welcome [well-advised] counsel (Proverbs 13:10 AMP).

COMMENTARY

Making presumptions (or assuming) is a roadblock. We must always be ready (and willing) to not only receive wise counsel but to give it as well. I was approached to start and lead a weekly journaling program at my library. I had never even thought about doing this (but later realized it was part of God's plan for me). When I prayed about it, the Lord said to say yes, so I did. We cannot presume because we don't have the exact qualifications, we cannot plant a seed where God is calling us to. Why? Because we do not know the outcome. The scripture says, "God qualifies the unqualified" (1 Corinthians 2:1-5). The program lasted over one year, and I have been able to counsel and pray with members. At least three of the members were Christians, and we were able to share encouragement and wisdom. We must know God's Word, meditate on it daily, and pray for His wisdom so we will be ready when He gives us opportunities. God bless.

What did God reveal to you through today's devotion?

_____

_____

_____

_____

_____

114. Why Give Thanks

Good morning entrepreneurs,

O give thanks unto the Lord; for he is good: because his mercy endureth for ever (Psalm 118:1 AMP).

COMMENTARY

God never promised believers would live an easy life, but He does promise our hardships aren't in vain. Everything that happens in our lives is an opportunity for us to give thanks to God. Why? Because He is with us through every trial we endure. He never leaves us; He never forsakes us. We give thanks for the mind and body He has blessed us with and the strength to create and grow our business. What have you given thanks to God for today? God bless.

What did God reveal to you through today's devotion?

_____

_____

_____

_____

_____

_____

_____

_____

_____

_____

115. Be Careful How You Respond

Good morning entrepreneurs,

And whoever forces you to go one mile, go with him two (Matt. 5:41 AMP).

COMMENTARY

Sometimes people will try to force you to do things you don't want to, but be discerning. There are times agreeing to do it and going the extra mile can be a blessing to you and to the person you respond to in a caring and compassionate way. Don't allow others to push your buttons. Hold on to the fruit of peace and patience and see how God will use you! God bless.

What did God reveal to you through today's devotion?

_____

_____

_____

_____

_____

_____

_____

_____

_____

_____

_____

_____

116. Always Do Your Best

Good morning entrepreneurs,

Whatever you do [whatever your task may be], work from the soul [that is, put in your very best effort], as [something done] for the Lord and not for men, knowing [with all certainty] that it is from the Lord [not from men] that you will receive the inheritance which is your [greatest] reward. It is the Lord Christ whom you [actually] serve (Colossians 3:23-24 AMP).

COMMENTARY

There was a day I wasn't feeling well but had an assignment at church. I was driving to church, and my husband called saying I should come back home and rest. I told him I couldn't do that because I was on an assignment for the Lord. I was able to complete the assignment, then go by the store. I expected comments from my husband when I got home, but I prayed before going in and everything was fine. As I reflected on the day later, I was reminded, "Only what we do for Christ will last." The above scripture is the reference for that statement. Don't allow anyone to take you from the assignment God has given you, even if they seem to have your best interest in mind. People will try to insert what they think is good for you, with good intentions, but if you are doing something for the Lord, stay steadfast and complete your assignment and God will handle the rest! God bless.

Write about a time someone tried to "detour" you from God's assignment. How did you handle it and what was the outcome?

---

117. How Strong Are You?

Good morning entrepreneurs,
And blessed [spiritually fortunate and favored by God] is she who believed and confidently trusted that there would be a fulfillment of the things that were spoken to her [by the angel sent] from the Lord (Luke 1:45 AMP).

COMMENTARY

Eleanor Roosevelt said, "Women are like teabags; you never know how strong they are until you put them in hot water." As women (and men) of God, no matter how hot the water we are in, God is there to lead, guide, and direct us. Our responsibility is to make sure it is the Lord's voice we are hearing, then to be obedient. God bless.

Are you being put in "hot water?" How are you dealing with it?

_____

_____

_____

_____

_____

_____

_____

_____

_____

_____

_____

118. Your Way is Not My Way

Good morning entrepreneurs,

I wish that all the people were as I am; but each person has his own gift from God, one of this kind and one of that (1 Corinthians 7:7 AMP).

COMMENTARY

Jesus does not expect us to be perfect as He was, but He does expect us to know what our gift is and ask God to help us walk in and perfect it. Our business flows out of our gift. Your gift is usually the skill or service you don't like doing, but God has equipped you to do it in excellence and it will become your passion. Here is a link for a spiritual gifts test: https://giftstest.com/. God bless.

What did God reveal to you through today's devotion?

_____

_____

_____

_____

_____

_____

_____

_____

_____

_____

_____

119. Your Gift is Not Mine

Good morning entrepreneurs,

Just as each one of you has received a special gift [a spiritual talent, an ability graciously given by God], employ it in serving one another as [is appropriate for] good stewards of God's multi-faceted grace [faithfully using the diverse, varied gifts and abilities granted to Christians by God's unmerited favor] (1 Peter 4:10).

Yesterday's devotion talked about how Christ doesn't expect us to be perfect as He was. Today's scripture reminds us we each have a *special* gift. We can't look at what others do and wish we could do what they are doing. Why? Because their gift is not ours. You are required to grow and make use of the gift God has deposited in you and I am to do the same. Stay in your lane and cultivate your gift, looking inside yourself and not at others. Don't spend so much time envying the gifts of others that you overlook your own! God bless.

What did God reveal to you through today's devotion?

_____

_____

_____

_____

_____

_____

_____

_____

120. Are You Talking or Doing?

Good morning entrepreneurs,

In all labor there is profit, but mere talk leads only to poverty (Proverbs 14:23 AMP).

COMMENTARY

My mom used to say, " Talk is cheap."

I have learned to do less talking about what I am doing and focus on the doing. The results will speak for themselves, and I can then give credit to God for what He allowed and helped me to do. What happens when you do more listening than talking? Try it! God bless.

What did God reveal to you through today's devotion?

_____

_____

_____

_____

_____

_____

_____

_____

_____

_____

_____

121. Don't Be Afraid to Speak Up

Good morning entrepreneurs,

Without consultation and wise advice, plans are frustrated, but with many counselors they are established and succeed (Proverbs 15:22 AMP).

Yesterday's devotion talked about listening more than talking. Today's devotion says to speak up. Please allow me to clarify. I watched an episode of *The Tamron Hall Show* on May 4, 2022. Nia Dennis, an American gymnast, was a guest and talked about how she would like to be on *Dancing with the Stars.* Cheryl Burke was also a guest and Tamron Hall said she was going to connect them. Connections are such an important part of our business success. God will connect us to the people and wise counsel we need to make our business successful. First, we must ask the Lord to direct us. Second, we must talk about our business and speak about our desires to others when we are led to speak. You never know when someone is listening who can help you. Third, don't be afraid to step out and be obedient when God is leading you to do something new. If He is guiding you, you may fall but you will not fail. Falling teaches lessons that lead to success. Speaking up involves speaking as God leads you. God bless.

What did God reveal to you through today's devotion?

_____

_____

_____

_____

_____

122. Who is Your Neighbor?

Good morning entrepreneurs,

'And you shall love the Lord your God with all your heart, and with all your soul (life), and with all your mind (thought, understanding), and with all your strength.' This is the second: 'You shall [unselfishly] love your neighbor as yourself.' There is no other commandment greater than these (Mark 12:30-31 AMP).

COMMENTARY

I was reading this scripture as part of my devotion yesterday. I have read it countless times, but I asked the Lord, "Who is my neighbor?" Suddenly, it was as if the response was, "Your neighbor is everyone but you!" This really put this scripture in perspective for me, and I hope it will for you as well. God bless.

What did God reveal to you through today's devotion?

_____

_____

_____

_____

_____

_____

_____

_____

_____

_____

123. Measure Your Level of Maturity

Good morning entrepreneurs,
When a man's ways please the Lord, he makes even his enemies to be at peace with him (Proverbs 16:7).

COMMENTARY

Mature people don't allow things to upset them. They have a quiet, accepting spirit. Even when things upset them, you never know it. Understand, there is a difference between not being upset and suppressing something that upsets you. Maturity says we take the things that upset us to God, and He will put it in the proper perspective for us. Just trust, believe, and wait patiently on God's response. God bless.

What are two things God recently revealed to you that you could have done differently?

_____

_____

_____

_____

_____

_____

_____

_____

_____

124. Nothing is Small

Good morning entrepreneurs,

Who [with reason] despises the day of small things (beginnings)? For these seven [eyes] shall rejoice when they see the plumb line in the hand of Zerubbabel. They are the eyes of the Lord which roam throughout the earth (Zachariah 4:10 AMP).

COMMENTARY

The early days of your business are when seeds are sown, and foundations are laid. Celebrate every small victory for, if you persevere, you will reap the dividends and the blessings will overflow. Remember the sowing and reaping process is continual. Small seeds sown reap tremendous rewards. What seeds are you sowing? God bless.

What did God reveal to you through today's devotion?

_____

_____

_____

_____

_____

_____

_____

_____

_____

_____

125. The Mindset of a Godly Entrepreneur

Good morning entrepreneurs,

For who has known the mind of the Lord, that He will instruct him? But we have the mind of Christ (1 Corinthians 2:16).

COMMENTARY

We do not know God's mind. God has, however, given us the Holy Spirit who directs us on how to live according to what God wants us to know for our lives. Our mindset must be not to do what we think, but to do what the Holy Spirit directs us to do. Are you excited about your business? Do you really believe you can start and successfully run your business? It's time for a "Mindset Check." What is your mindset about your business? God bless.

What did God reveal to you through today's devotion?

_____

_____

_____

_____

_____

_____

_____

_____

_____

_____

126. Grow Your Business Step by Step

Good morning entrepreneurs,

Let your eyes look directly ahead [toward the path of moral courage] And let your gaze be fixed straight in front of you [toward the path of integrity]. Consider well and carefully watch the path of your feet, and all your ways will be steadfast and sure (Proverbs 4:25-26 AMP).

COMMENTARY

As you structure and grow your business, don't be discouraged by what you didn't do yesterday. Make corrections when needed, then start fresh each day, staying on the path God has for you, and making sure to follow the rules of morality and integrity. How do you remain steadfast with integrity in your business? God bless.

What did God reveal to you through today's devotion?

_____

_____

_____

_____

_____

_____

_____

_____

_____

_____

_____

127. God is Our Rock

Good morning entrepreneurs,
My flesh and my heart may fail, But God is the rock and strength of my heart and my portion forever (Psalm 73:26 AMP).

COMMENTARY

Today you may feel like there is no way that you can do all that is necessary for your business. Tomorrow you may wake up and feel like everything is working according to plan. Remember, God is strengthening us to do what He has called us to do. Don't follow your body or your feelings. There were times I thought I was too old to continue my business. Then God would give me a completely new branch of my business to pursue. With His help and strength, I have persevered. He will help you in the same way. Believe that He is your rock and will give you what you need to keep going. How has God been your rock in your business? God bless.

What did God reveal to you through today's devotion?

_____

_____

_____

_____

_____

_____

_____

128. Believe in God Not Our Fears

Good morning entrepreneurs,

Overhearing what was being said, Jesus said to the synagogue official, "Do not be afraid; only keep on believing [in Me and my power]" (Mark 5:36 AMP).

COMMENTARY

When we confess our sins to God, ask for forgiveness and allow our belief in Jesus and His power to keep us going, we will begin to see the blessings of success in our business. Take some time today to honestly face your sins and confess them to God. Let us remember when Jesus arose from the dead on Resurrection Sunday, He not only overcame death, but He also overcame every sin we would commit. God bless.

What did God reveal to you through today's devotion?

_____

_____

_____

_____

_____

_____

_____

_____

_____

_____

129. The Art of Faithful Work

Good morning entrepreneurs,
For the word of the Lord is right; And all His work is done in faithfulness
(Psalm 33:4 AMP).

COMMENTARY

Take a few minutes today to reflect on God's faithfulness to you.
Name four ways that you have been blessed in your business this year.
God bless.

What did God reveal to you through today's devotion?

_____

_____

_____

_____

_____

_____

_____

_____

_____

_____

_____

_____

130. Continually Examine Yourself

Good morning entrepreneurs,

But each one must carefully scrutinize his own work [examining his actions, attitudes, and behavior], and then he can have the personal satisfaction and inner joy of doing something commendable without comparing himself to another (Galatians 6:4 AMP).

COMMENTARY

Sometimes we ask ourselves, "Am I doing something wrong? Why are others' businesses so prosperous while I am struggling to get mine off the ground?" I read an amazing book by Pastor T.D. Jakes titled, *Planted for a Purpose*. One of the many truths he said was, "Quality takes time." He's not referring to our time, but to God's time. He talks about the time it takes for grapes to turn into wine and the fermentation process. Looking at the success of others and comparing it to ours only causes frustration and discouragement. Instead, ask God to show you what is standing in the way of your success. If you spend enough quiet time in His presence, He will reveal it to you. Then, be obedient to His direction. What is God saying about the season of your success? God bless.

What did God reveal to you through today's devotion?

_____

_____

_____

_____

_____

_____

131. Watch Your Words

Good morning entrepreneurs,

Understand this, my beloved brothers, and sisters. Let everyone be quick to hear [be a careful, thoughtful listener], slow to speak [a speaker of carefully chosen words and], slow to anger [patient, reflective, forgiving] (James 1:19 AMP).

COMMENTARY

As a businessperson, you must acquire the ability to listen more than you speak. It takes focus because we always want to make sure that we get "Our" point across. At the same time if we don't listen to our customer, we may miss an opportunity to retain a client, and even more important, to minister to someone. Remember, we have two ears but only one mouth. As we plant our seeds, make sure we take time to listen to the other person because we may learn something!

What did God reveal to you through today's devotion?

_____

_____

_____

_____

_____

_____

_____

_____

_____

132. Get Out of the Boat

Good morning entrepreneurs,

Peter replied to Him, "Lord, if it is [really] You, command me to come to You on the water." He said, "Come!]" So, Peter got out of the boat, and walked on the water and came toward Jesus (Matthew 14:28-29 AMP).

COMMENTARY

Do you believe Jesus is calling you to "get out of the boat" to do something that is completely out of your comfort zone for your business? Then what are you waiting for? Know that Jesus is there to catch you if you fall, but if you never step out of your boat of normalcy and routine, you will never experience the exciting things God has planned for you. So.....Step out! Question, what is your "Get out of the boat" assignment? God bless.

What did God reveal to you through today's devotion?

_____

_____

_____

_____

_____

_____

_____

_____

_____

133. Tests Will Increase Your Strength

Good morning entrepreneurs,

Be assured that the testing of your faith [through experience] produces endurance [leading to spiritual maturity, and inner peace]. And let endurance have its perfect result and do a thorough work, so that you may be perfect and completely developed [in your faith], lacking in nothing (James 1:3-4 AMP).

COMMENTARY

Sometimes, no matter how strong we are in the Lord, we have weak moments, times of doubt and a low faith level. The scripture above says that we are being tested during these times and we must endure. Remember God's past blessings in your life. Remember that you are His child, and He is always with you. This is an opportunity for you to step back, trust God, and watch Him work another miracle in your life. Be patient, endure (stand strong without yielding), and trust the Lord. God bless.

What was your most recent test and how did you endure?

_____

_____

_____

_____

_____

_____

_____

_____

134. Creating the Business God Wants

Good morning entrepreneurs,

He must increase [in prominence], but I must decrease (John 3:30 AMP).

COMMENTARY

As we ask God to guide us in our business, it must be less about what we believe we need to do and more about what God is urging us to do. One of my favorite scriptures is Matthew 6:33; "But first and most importantly seek (aim at, strive after) His kingdom and His righteousness [His way of doing and being right—the attitude and character of God], and all these things will be given to you also." Do what the Holy Spirit is leading you to do FIRST, and the Lord will take care of everything else! What change is God showing you for your business? God bless.

What did God reveal to you through today's devotion?

_____

_____

_____

_____

_____

_____

_____

_____

_____

135. Look Back with Joy

Good morning, entrepreneurs

Every branch in Me that does not bear fruit, He takes away; and every branch that continues to bear fruit, He [repeatedly] prunes, so that it will bear more fruit [even richer and finer fruit] (John 15:2).

COMMENTARY

In Phase 1, we focused on breaking. This devotion is a review to see how God's breaking process has changed you. Every "Friend" we lose, every disappointment, every difficulty in relationships, every close person in our life who passes away, every time we feel hopeless, every business opportunity that fails is all part of our pruning process. We may not like it at the time, but when we look back later, we will see these difficulties drew us closer to God. They also caused us to be more fruitful. Don't despise God's process! God bless.

Take a minute to write how God has "pruned" you since the beginning of this devotional journey.

_____

_____

_____

_____

_____

_____

_____

_____

136. Put Your Gift to Work

Good morning entrepreneurs,

Do not neglect the spiritual gift within you, [that special endowment] which was intentionally bestowed on you [by the Holy Spirit] through prophetic utterance when the elders laid their hands on you [at your ordination] (1 Timothy 4:14 AMP).

COMMENTARY

I can't encourage you enough to put your spiritual gift to work. Your business is your spiritual gift and every aspect of it. If you took the spiritual assessment test recommended in an earlier devotion, you have identified your gifts. Now the question is, are you putting them to work? What gifts are you pausing on because you are not sure you can do it? Write them here, then ask God to give you the courage to begin using it. God bless.

What did God reveal to you through today's devotion?

_____

_____

_____

_____

_____

_____

_____

_____

_____

137. What Does Your Character Look Like?

Good morning entrepreneurs,

Let your character [your moral essence, your inner nature] be free from the love of money [shun greed—be financially ethical], being content with what you have; for He has said, "I will never [under any circumstances] desert you [nor give you up nor leave you without support, nor will I in any degree leave you helpless], nor will I forsake or let you down or relax My hold on you [assuredly not]" (Hebrews 13:5 AMP)!

COMMENTARY

To be content does not mean you remain stagnant. To be content is to be satisfied where we are right now because we know that the Lord is always watching over us; He will never leave or forsake us. He will provide all our needs and some of our desires as they fit into His plan for our lives.

Being content means: not being afraid, not being anxious, not being disappointed, not being discouraged, not being angry, not having regret, not being compulsive, not having doubt, not giving up, not procrastinating, and/or not being jealous. So, how content are you in this planting and cultivating phase? What does your character look like and where does it need to change? God bless.

What did God reveal to you through today's devotion?

_____

_____

_____

_____

_____

138. Don't Stop Planning

Good morning entrepreneurs,

Many plans are in a man's mind, but it is the Lord's purpose for him that will stand [be carried out] (Proverbs 19:21 AMP).

Yes, we are still talking about planning. It is so crucial to the success of your business to plan then go to God and adjust it according to His plan and purpose. It is not our plans that will make us successful in our business; it is knowing God's purpose for us and our business, and establishing our plans according to His purpose and the purpose for our business that will make us successful. How is your business plan progressing? Is it time for an adjustment? God bless.

What did God reveal to you through today's devotion?

_____

_____

_____

_____

_____

_____

_____

_____

_____

_____

_____

139. The Beauty of Kindness

Good morning entrepreneurs,

He has told you, "O man, what is good? And what does the Lord require of you except to be just, and to love [and to diligently practice] kindness (compassion), and to walk humbly with your God [setting aside any overblown sense of importance or self-righteousness]" (Micah 6:8 AMP)?

COMMENTARY

God expects us to be just (fair), kind, and walk humbly with Him. It sounds easy but to have these attributes every minute of every day takes discipline, prayer, and constant focus on God. Ask God to help you grow in these areas daily. What do you need to do to be a kinder, humbler person? God bless.

What did God reveal to you through today's devotion?

_____

_____

_____

_____

_____

_____

_____

_____

_____

_____

_____

140. Watch God's Timing Not Your Circumstances

Good morning entrepreneurs,

He who watches the wind [waiting for all conditions to be perfect] will not sow [seed], and he who looks at the clouds will not reap [a harvest] (Ecclesiastes 11:4 AMP).

As we work to build our business, we may think we must wait for the right time, sufficient finances, the right office space, the right opportunity. This scripture tells us, don't wait for the perfect situation, prayerfully begin with what you have. When you begin to work with the tools God has already provided, He will expand them. Even when waiting, it is an active process with God. He is showing you what you must do while waiting. What is God showing you about tools you already have to move your business forward? God bless.

What did God reveal to you through today's devotion?

_____

_____

_____

_____

_____

_____

_____

_____

_____

_____

141. Moving with God

Good morning entrepreneurs,
I will instruct you and teach you in the way you should go. I will counsel you [who are willing to learn] with My eye upon you (Psalm 32:8 AMP).

COMMENTARY

In T.D. Jakes's book, *Planted for a Purpose,* he says, "God is always on the move." In the same way, to be in the likeness of Christ means we should always be on the move. Even when we are waiting for God to speak to us, we should be actively reading His Word and praying for His instruction. We are not impulsively, blindly moving ahead. We are asking, seeking, knocking, reading, and praying for instructions. God bless.

How are you waiting on God for your next step?

_____

_____

_____

_____

_____

_____

_____

_____

_____

_____

142. The Principle of How to Treat Others

Good morning entrepreneurs,

So then, in everything treat others the same way you want them to treat you, for this is [the essence of] the Law and the [writings of the] Prophets (Matthew 7:12 AMP).

COMMENTARY

This scripture has been the guiding principle for my etiquette business since I started in 2001, but the Holy Spirit revealed it to me in a new way. I had grandma duty to pick up my 4-year-old granddaughter from preschool. When I arrived at my daughter's house, there was a sink full of dishes (she is a very busy lady). She apologized for how the house looked as she came upstairs from her office. We talked for a few minutes, and she went back to work. As I walked into the kitchen, I remembered my life at this stage. I thought how amazing it would have been if someone would have cleaned my kitchen and tidied up my house. I had enough time to start before picking up my granddaughter, so that's what I did. When we arrived back home, I finished up and my granddaughter and I made a game of "Pickup" to tidy the house. The words of appreciation and look in my daughter's eyes gave me so much joy! As you go through each day, what are ways we can help others? Being obedient will give joy to them and you! God bless.

What did God reveal to you through today's devotion?

_____

_____

_____

_____

_____

143. The Privilege of Approaching God

Good morning, entrepreneurs

Therefore, let us [with privilege] approach the throne of grace [that is, the throne of God's gracious favor] with confidence and without fear, so that we may receive mercy [for our failures] and find [His amazing] grace to help in time of need [an appropriate blessing, coming just at the right moment] (Hebrews 4:16).

COMMENTARY

God is always there waiting for us to come to Him. Allow this morning's devotion to draw you to God's throne of grace to worship and praise Him for who He is. God bless.

What did God reveal to you through today's devotion?

_____

_____

_____

_____

_____

_____

_____

_____

_____

_____

_____

144. God's Strong Tower

Good morning entrepreneurs,

The name of the Lord is a strong tower. The righteous runs to it and is safe and set on high [far above evil] (Proverbs 18:10).

Trust in the name of the Lord to protect, strengthen, give peace, and whatever you need in life. The name of the Lord is the strongest power we have or could ever have! God bless.

What will you ask for in the name of Jesus today?

_____

_____

_____

_____

_____

_____

_____

_____

_____

_____

_____

_____

_____

145. Idleness is a Deterrent

Good morning entrepreneurs,
Poor is he who works with a negligent and idle hand, but the hand of the diligent makes him rich (Proverbs 10:4 AMP).

COMMENTARY

We all need rest because we have so many things going on. It seems though, the things of the world put demands and time constraints on us (our job, appointments, etc.), but the things of God do not. In reality, the things of God are much more important and should be our priority. Your business is one of the things God has assigned to you, your specific gift for a specific purpose. How much time have you spent developing your business in the last month? We tell God how grateful we are for His blessings, but then we are slack in growing the business He has blessed us with. What can you do today to grow your business? God bless.

What did God reveal to you through today's devotion?

_____

_____

_____

_____

_____

_____

_____

_____

146. How to Be Grounded

Good morning entrepreneurs,

Therefore, my beloved brothers and sisters, be steadfast, immovable, always excelling in the work of the Lord [always doing your best and doing more than is needed], being continually aware that your labor [even to the point of exhaustion] in the Lord is not futile nor wasted [it is never without purpose] (1 Corinthians 15:58 AMP).

COMMENTARY

Part of being steadfast in your business is taking every opportunity to learn and "seek first the things of God." How are you seeking God for your business? (Matt 6:33). God bless.

What did God reveal to you through today's devotion?

_____

_____

_____

_____

_____

_____

_____

_____

_____

_____

_____

_____

147. Talking About Fear…. Again

Good morning entrepreneurs,

Do not fear [anything], for I am with you. Do not be afraid, for I am your God. I will strengthen you, be assured I will help you. I will certainly take hold of you with My righteous right hand [a hand of justice, of power, of victory, of salvation] (Isaiah 41:10 AMP).

When you are in business, you must put your name and face out there for others to see. This means doing interviews, podcasts, YouTube videos, and other marketing strategies. I don't know about you, but that scares me even now. What I want to share in this devotion is doing any work for the Lord can be scary. We may feel inadequate, ignorant, and lost. Actually, this is all true! This devotion is to remind you once again that when God gives us an assignment, He gives us the tools to accomplish it. Sometimes, we have difficulty distinguishing His words from our thoughts and we make mistakes. That's okay because mistakes are part of the process to teach us and keep us humble while He is molding, breaking, and pruning us in every step of the process. Whatever assignment God has blessed you to do, know that He is there strengthening you, helping you, and holding your hand. Don't let the enemy talk you out of doing God's work. Don't be afraid to put one foot in front of the other and trust Him. What are you fearful of today? God bless.

What did God reveal to you through today's devotion?

_____

_____

_____

_____

148. Don't Stray from the Path

Good morning entrepreneurs,

Establish my footsteps in [the way of] Your Word. Do not let any human weakness have power over me [causing me to be separated from You] (Psalm 119:133 AMP)

COMMENTARY

This is one of my favorite scriptures I pray each morning. If God is ordering (establishing) our steps, there is no need to worry about our day. Make a schedule, just know that God may have other plans and be ready to adjust. As God establishes our steps, He perfects our daily schedule. God bless.

What steps are being established by God for you today?

_____

_____

_____

_____

_____

_____

_____

_____

_____

_____

_____

149. How to Work Smart Not Hard

Good morning entrepreneurs,

But by the [remarkable] grace of God I am what I am, and His grace toward me was not without effect. In fact, I worked harder than all of the apostles, though it was not I, but the grace of God [His unmerited favor and blessing which was] with me (1 Corinthians 15:10 AMP).

COMMENTARY

We can be motivated by passion, fear, love, a sense of accomplishment, deadlines, etc. When I read this scripture, I was reminded that I am what I am only because of God. What drives and motivates me (and should do the same for you) to work and serve in the Kingdom of God is my love for God and what He has done for me. Take a minute to think about where you were 10, 25, 30 years ago. Now take another minute to see how God's hand was there every step of the way and how He has blessed us.

Now, get busy working and serving for the Kingdom through your business to help someone else to know God or know Him more intimately, so they can experience His love, mercy, and blessings. God bless.

What is your next serving assignment?

_____

_____

_____

_____

_____

_____

150. The Sufficiency of God

Good morning entrepreneurs,

But He has said to me, "My grace is sufficient for you [My lovingkindness and My mercy are more than enough—always available—regardless of the situation]; for [My] power is being perfected [and is completed and shows itself most effectively] in [your] weakness. Therefore, I will all the more gladly boast in my weaknesses, so that the power of Christ [may completely enfold me and] may dwell in me" (2 Corinthians 12:9 AMP).

COMMENTARY

When we are at our weakest, our lowest—struggling with health, financial issues, family problems, discouragement, etc.—that is when God's strength takes over. If you are dealing with problems in any of these areas or others, surrender to God and confess your weakness. Then thank God for His strength and mercy. Trust Him, because there is a breakthrough and a blessing on the way. God bless.

Where is your weakest area right now?

_____

_____

_____

_____

_____

_____

_____

_____

_____

151. What/Whom Do You Put Your Trust in?

Good morning entrepreneurs

Some trust in chariots and some in horses, but we will remember and trust in the name of the Lord our God (Psalm 20:7 AMP).

COMMENTARY

People trust in many things; jobs, bank accounts, people, and more. But only the Lord will help us and rescue us from any situation in our lives. Trust in Him and Him alone for whatever you need. God bless.

In whom (or what) do you trust?

_____

_____

_____

_____

_____

_____

_____

_____

_____

_____

_____

_____

_____

152. Stop Comparing Yourself

Good morning entrepreneurs,

So then, my dear ones, just as you have always obeyed [my instructions with enthusiasm], not only in my presence, but now much more in my absence, continue to work out your salvation [that is, cultivate it, bring it to full effect, actively pursue spiritual maturity] with awe-inspired fear and trembling [using serious caution and critical self-evaluation to avoid anything that might offend God or discredit the name of Christ] (Philippians 2:12 AMP).

COMMENTARY

Stop comparing yourself to others!

I heard a sermon yesterday and the pastor said, "We need to stop comparing ourselves to others. When I compare myself to others, I hinder myself." The world causes us to compare ourselves to each other, but we don't know what is behind that seemingly successful life. Our life may not look so successful in the eyes of others (or to ourselves). On the other hand, others may see our lives as more successful than theirs. We must remember that we are God's children, and He is the one who determines our success according to His Word and His plan for our lives. God bless.

In what ways do you compare yourself to others?

_____

_____

_____

_____

_____

_____

153. Displaying Courtesy

Good morning entrepreneurs,
To slander or abuse no one, to be kind and conciliatory and gentle, showing unqualified consideration and courtesy toward everyone (Titus 3:2 AMP).

COMMENTARY

Courtesy, a character we should always display but especially in our business. Courtesy can help you increase your clientele and avoid disputes and disagreements. The customer may not always be right, but the Word says they should still be treated with "unqualified consideration and courtesy." God bless.

How do you display courtesy to others?

_____

_____

_____

_____

_____

_____

_____

_____

_____

_____

_____

_____

154. Be Obstinate in Your Principles

Good morning entrepreneurs,

Therefore, [let me warn you] beloved, knowing these things beforehand, be on your guard so that you are not carried away by the error of unprincipled men [who distort doctrine] and fall from your own steadfastness [of mind, knowledge, truth, and faith], but grow [spiritually mature] in the grace and knowledge of our Lord and Savior Jesus Christ. To Him be glory (honor, majesty, splendor), both now and to the day of eternity. Amen (2 Peter 3:17-18 AMP).

COMMENTARY

Rolex, the most prestigious watch company in the world, has a quote that says, "Only the most obstinate are successful." To be obstinate means to be firmly or stubbornly adhering to one's purpose; inflexible persistence or steadfast.

Let us not let go, give up, lose heart, or become discouraged if the vision of our business does not progress as we expect. Let us be firmly planted in our conviction to it. The success will come according to God's timing, so don't give up! God bless.

What did God reveal to you through today's devotion?

_____

_____

_____

_____

_____

_____

_____

155. The Character of Steadfastness

Good morning entrepreneurs,

Consider well and carefully watch the path of your feet, and all your ways will be steadfast and sure. Do not turn away to the right nor to the left [where evil may lurk]. Turn your foot from [the path of] evil (Proverbs 4:26-27 AMP).

COMMENTARY

I was reading this scripture last night, and it reminded me again of the importance of being steadfast. Did you know the word steadfast is mentioned 219 times in the Bible? That gives us an idea of how important that word is in our lives. God knew we would need to see it again and again. It also tells us how easy it can be to lose the spirit of being steadfast because it is mentioned so many times. The more steadfast we become, the more likely we are to accomplish our life's purpose and the more peaceful and joyful our lives will be. God bless.

How steadfast are you?

_____

_____

_____

_____

_____

_____

_____

_____

_____

156. Continue in Steadfastness

Good morning entrepreneurs,

Be on guard; stand firm in your faith [in God, respecting His precepts and keeping your doctrine sound]. Act like [mature] men and be courageous; be strong. Let everything you do be done in love [motivated and inspired by God's love for us] (2 Corinthians 16:13-14 AMP).

COMMENTARY

We are still looking at the importance of being steadfast. Today's scripture tells us to be on guard, look out, be watchful, and pay attention. While you work on being steadfast, fixed with purpose, watch out for the things that try to take you off course. God bless.

What are two areas of your life that make you waver in your steadfastness?

_____

_____

_____

_____

_____

_____

_____

_____

_____

_____

157. Stand on Your Principles

Good morning entrepreneurs,
But let your statement be, 'Yes, yes' or 'No, no' [a firm yes or no]; anything more than that comes from the evil one (Matthew 5:37 AMP).

COMMENTARY

Three days ago, your devotion was to be obstinate in your principles (firmly adhering). Today is about letting others see you walking in those principles. Be firm in what you will and will not do. Don't allow the desire for success in your business cause you to change what you stand for. Lastly, if you say you will do something, make sure that you do it. If the Holy Spirit tells you to say no, don't waver or change your mind. Stand by your decision. How do you walk? God bless.

What did God reveal to you through today's devotion?

_____

_____

_____

_____

_____

_____

_____

_____

_____

_____

158. When You are Given Much, You are Required to Give Much in Return

Good morning entrepreneurs,

But the one who did not know it and did things worthy of a beating, will receive only a few [lashes]. From everyone to whom much has been given, much will be required; and to whom they entrusted much, of him they will ask all the more (Luke 12:48 AMP).

COMMENTARY

God has blessed us with so much! In return, He expects us to make an impact in the life of someone else. Each day we wake up is an opportunity to do something, not ordinary, but extraordinary for the Lord. Experience has taught me that I must ask Him each day for the opportunity to make an impact in the life of another person. Once I ask, I must be alert for opportunities (because He will send them in the most unlikely way and time). God bless.

Did you make an impact in someone's life today? Write your experience below.

_____

_____

_____

_____

_____

_____

_____

_____

159. Spread Your Gift!

Good morning entrepreneurs,

That is why I remind you to fan into flame the gracious gift of God, [that inner fire—the special endowment] which is in you through the laying on of my hands [with those of the elders at your ordination]. For God did not give us a spirit of timidity or cowardice or fear, but [He has given us a spirit] of power and of love and of sound judgment and personal discipline [abilities that result in a calm, well-balanced mind, and self-control] (2 Timothy 1:6-7).

COMMENTARY

Recently, the elder in my church called me to say she was speaking to someone who wanted to have a church etiquette workshop. The elder connected me with the person, and I prayerfully prepared to facilitate a Zoom church etiquette workshop on "Kingdom Courtesy: Church Etiquette Before, During and After Covid." I have facilitated hundreds of workshops, but I must admit I was battling with a spirit of fear. The scripture above reminds us that we must "fan into the flame the gift God has placed in us." We must push past the fear, and prayerfully ask God to fill us with His power to accomplish the assignment we have been given to use our gift. The workshop was successful because of my obedience. I share this to encourage you to push forward, fanning the flame of your gift for the Lord. God bless.

What did God reveal to you through today's devotion?

_____

_____

_____

_____

160. The Gift of Our Business

Good morning entrepreneurs,
Now we who are strong [in our convictions and faith] ought to [patiently] put up with the weaknesses of those who are not strong, and not just please ourselves (Romans 15:1 AMP).

COMMENTARY

Remember our business was not given to us for us, but to be a blessing to someone else. Ask God for opportunities to offer complimentary products and services to others. You will help others, and it will lead to blessings/opportunities for you. We are blessed when we bless others. God bless.

Who can you bless today through your business?

_____

_____

_____

_____

_____

_____

_____

_____

_____

_____

161. The Concept of Sowing and Reaping

Good morning entrepreneurs,

There is the one who [generously] scatters [abroad], and yet increases all the more; And there is the one who withholds what is justly due, but it results only in want and poverty. The generous man [is a source of blessing and] shall be prosperous and enriched, and he who waters will himself be watered [reaping the generosity he has sown]. The people curse him who holds back grain [when the public needs it], but a blessing [from God and man] is upon the head of him who sells it. He who diligently seeks good seeks favor and grace, but he who seeks evil, evil will come to him. He who leans on and trusts in and is confident in his riches will fall, but the righteous [who trust in God's provision] will flourish like a green leaf (Proverbs 11:24-28(AMP).

COMMENTARY

Today is a continued conversation about blessing others. When we give complimentary products or services, don't consider it as losing money, consider it as being obedient to God's command of generosity. Whatever we are led to give, don't hesitate. As we bless others, God blesses and provides for us! God bless.

What did God reveal to you through today's devotion?

_____

_____

_____

_____

_____

_____

_____

162. Close Your Eyes

Good morning entrepreneurs,

I will lead the blind by a way they do not know; I will guide them in paths that they do not know. I will make darkness into light before them and rugged places into plains. These things I will do [for them], And I will not leave them abandoned or undone (Isaiah 42:16 AMP).

COMMENTARY

If we close our eyes and blindly trust God, He will guide us to places that we didn't even know existed, and He will be with us every step of the journey. When God presents new opportunities in our business, don't be afraid to step out on faith. By doing so, you will step into unimaginable blessings! God bless.

What do you need to close your eyes and trust God for?

_____

_____

_____

_____

_____

_____

_____

_____

_____

_____

_____

4th Phase – Walking in Newness of a Godly Entrepreneur

Your eyes have been opened, you have allowed God to remove the things that needed to be broken, and the ground in your heart is being cultivated. You have made it to the final phase of this journey to success on your knees! This final phase is learning how to walk in your newness as a new creature, a godly entrepreneur for the Lord. As you journey through this final phase of devotions, consider what God has taken you through these last seven months. Write it down so that when times are difficult (and there will still be some difficult times), you can reflect on this journey, remember your "Newness", and praise God to continue to take you through.

163. Seek God's Thoughts Daily

Good morning entrepreneurs,

The things which you have learned and received and heard and seen in me, practice these things [in daily life], and the God [who is the source] of peace and well-being will be with you (Philippians 4:9 AMP).

COMMENTARY

To be successful, we must strive each day to have the mind of Christ, the heart of Christ, and do those things Christ did. It is all laid out for us in His Word. Let us read it daily and ask God to order our steps to be obedient to what it says. How often do you read God's Word? God bless.

What did God reveal to you through today's devotion?

_____

_____

_____

_____

_____

_____

_____

_____

_____

_____

_____

164. Decrease My Thoughts/Increase God's Thoughts

Good morning entrepreneurs,

He must increase [in prominence], but I must decrease (John 3:30 AMP).

COMMENTARY

When God gives us an assignment—whether it is a speaking engagement, facilitating a workshop, encouraging, or leading a group session—we must decrease, and God must increase in us. Our mind, thoughts, heart, and actions must be surrendered to Him. We must read His Word and pray for direction and instruction. Next, we must prepare. Then we must bring our preparation before the Lord so that He can show us any necessary changes. Lastly, before we begin to speak, we must ask God (as John the Baptist did in the scripture above) to increase in us, so we will decrease. God bless.

What did God reveal to you through today's devotion?

_____

_____

_____

_____

_____

_____

_____

_____

165. Don't Doubt Your Calling

Good morning entrepreneurs,

But Jesus looked at them and said, "With people (as far as it depends on them) it is impossible, but with God all things are possible]" (Matthew 19:26 AMP).

For with God nothing [is or ever] shall be impossible (Luke 1:37 AMP).

COMMENTARY

Jesus said it TWICE in two different books! Why do we doubt the assignments God gives us when we know if we surrender to Him, there is nothing we can't accomplish? Stand on God's Word, surrender yourself. Then step out as He instructs you to be a blessing to others and give God the glory! God bless.

What did God reveal to you through today's devotion?

_____

_____

_____

_____

_____

_____

_____

_____

_____

_____

166. Thoughts and Attitudes of Christ

Good morning entrepreneurs,

Have this same attitude in yourselves which was in Christ Jesus [look to Him as your example in selfless humility] (Philippians 2:5 AMP).

COMMENTARY

If we are to be successful in our business, family, and life, we must pray to show others the mind of Christ working in us. We must never get to the point where we think, "I've got this" because that is when we fall and when the enemy can get a toehold in our lives. God bless.

What did God reveal to you through today's devotion?

_____

_____

_____

_____

_____

_____

_____

_____

_____

_____

_____

_____

167. Waiting with Patience

Good morning entrepreneurs,

Indeed, none of those who [expectantly] wait for You will be ashamed. Those who turn away from what is right and deal treacherously without cause will be ashamed (humiliated, embarrassed) (Psalm 25:3 AMP).

COMMENTARY

Patience is one of the fruits I honestly struggle with. Waiting on God is not easy. We want to see our business and the things we ask God for to come to fruition when we think they should. But we must remember, our ways are not God's ways. There are many flaws in our timing (as we have seen over our lives). God's timing for our life is perfect and includes everything we will ever go through. When we pray for patience, God will put situations in our lives that require us to be patient. Sometimes it will take years, but if we wait on God, our prayers will be answered and we will have a closer relationship with Him as a result. God bless.

How is your patience?

_____

_____

_____

_____

_____

_____

_____

168. Allow Your Business to Be a Blessing

Good morning entrepreneurs,

In all things I have shown you that by working hard in this way we must help the weak and remember the words of the Lord Jesus, how he himself said, "It is more blessed to give than to receive" (Acts 20:35 AMP).

COMMENTARY

In more than 20 years of being in business, although I have done some marketing, most of my clients have been by referral. I am not wealthy, but so many people have shared with me how my services, workshops, and books have been a blessing to them. Financially, the Lord always sends a new client or a new opportunity to me when I need a financial blessing. Some godly businesspersons become independently wealthy, but it's not about comparing yourself to others; it's about what God wants to do in you through you and for you. When you allow your gifts and your business to bless others, God will bless you financially and with a spirit of joy. God bless.

How has your business been a blessing to others?

_____

_____

_____

_____

_____

_____

_____

169. Remember to Rest

Good morning entrepreneurs,

So there remains a [full and complete] Sabbath rest for the people of God. For the one who has once entered His rest has also rested from [the weariness and pain of] his [human] labors, just as God rested from [those labors uniquely] His own (Hebrews 4:9-10 AMP).

COMMENTARY

This devotion is another reminder that we must take time to rest. As we work, take care of our families, fulfill duties at church and work to build our business, we tend to forget one thing — rest. When do we rest? When was the last time you slept late? Maybe took a walk on the beach or in the park alone? Or took a day just to do nothing? Sunday may not even be a day of rest if you serve at church. Our mind and body need time to rest. That is when we refresh and rejuvenate so that we can move forward with a clear perspective. When we don't take time to rest, we become burned out and discouraged. God commands that we rest! Other scriptures on rest are Matthew 11:28-30, Psalm 4:8, and Psalm 127:2. Meditate on these scriptures and others. Then, look at your calendar, decide on a day of rest and post a "Do not disturb" sign in your house and on your phone and get some rest! God bless.

When was the last time you took an entire day to rest?

_____

_____

_____

_____

170. What You Believe in Your Heart is What Will Be

Good morning entrepreneurs,

For as he thinks in his heart, so is he [in behavior—one who manipulates]. He says to you, "Eat and drink," Yet his heart is not with you [but it is begrudging the cost] (Proverbs 23:7 AMP).

COMMENTARY

Today's thought is simple. If you believe God has given you an idea for a business and you believe it will be successful, then it will be. If you don't believe this, then you will not be successful. You may already be working in your business, say you have faith, but not feel successful. But, if your business is blessing the people God wants it to bless, then it is a success in God's eyes, and that is what matters. Ask God to show you if you are operating your business the way He wants and to show you what His will is for your business. How do you feel about your business in your heart? God bless.

What did God reveal to you through today's devotion?

_____

_____

_____

_____

_____

_____

_____

_____

171. The Benefits of Praising God

Good morning, entrepreneurs

Bless and affectionately praise the Lord, O my soul, and do not forget any of His benefits; Who forgives all your sins, who heals all your diseases; Who redeems your life from the pit, who crowns you [lavishly] with loving kindness and tender mercy (Psalm 103:2-4 AMP).

COMMENTARY

Let us not forget ALL the Lord's blessings to us. Take time, right now, to think about all God has done in your life. Now, Give Him Praise! God bless.

What did God reveal to you through today's devotion?

_____

_____

_____

_____

_____

_____

_____

_____

_____

_____

_____

172. Allow God's Will to Be Accomplished

Good morning entrepreneurs,

The Lord will accomplish that which concerns me. Your [unwavering] lovingkindness, O Lord, endures forever—Do not abandon the works of Your own hands (Psalm 138:8 AMP).

COMMENTARY

Don't be concerned that your business is not expanding as quickly as you think it should. Sometimes we feel we should come to a point where we can say, "I have finished building my business." Know that this is a continuing process. Even when you think it is completely established, God will show you another area in which to grow. Our business will never be completed but ever expanding and growing as we grow in the Lord and He reveals more of His vision to us. God bless.

What new area is God showing you to grow your business?

_____

_____

_____

_____

_____

_____

_____

_____

_____

173. Expect Your Territory to Expand

Good morning entrepreneurs,

You enlarge my steps under me, and my feet have not slipped (2 Samuel 22:37).

COMMENTARY

If you truly want your business to grow, memorize and believe this scripture. Repeat it often. You will begin to see expansion in your business. Ask God to enlarge your territory and trust Him that you will not slip. Watch Him work as He expands your business. God bless.

What did God reveal to you through today's devotion?

_____

_____

_____

_____

_____

_____

_____

_____

_____

_____

_____

_____

_____

174. God's Vision Keeps Your Business Alive!

Good morning entrepreneurs,

Where there is no vision [no redemptive revelation of God], the people perish; but he who keeps the law [of God, which includes that of man]—blessed (happy, fortunate, and enviable) is he (Proverbs 29:18 AMP).

COMMENTARY

Take some time today to review your notes on the vision God has given you for your business. Make sure you have not omitted any steps. Each step God gives you is important to complete before He gives you the next step. If you are not following His vision, your business cannot thrive or even survive. Spend time with God this week and ask Him to make the next level of His vision plain to you. God bless.

What did God reveal to you through today's devotion?

_____

_____

_____

_____

_____

_____

_____

_____

_____

_____

175. What's Next on Your Path?

Good morning entrepreneurs,
You will show me the path of life; In Your presence is fullness of joy; In Your right hand there are pleasures forevermore (Psalm 16:11 AMP).

COMMENTARY

What is the next step in the path of your life? In the path of your business? Does your business give you joy? Are you excited to continue building your business? These are all questions that you must ask yourself. Go before the Lord with your answers and ask Him to guide you according to His path. God bless.

What did God reveal to you through today's devotion?

_____

_____

_____

_____

_____

_____

_____

_____

_____

_____

_____

_____

176. Your Word is Your Bond

Good morning entrepreneurs,

When a man makes a vow to God or binds himself by an oath to do something, he must not break his word; he must do exactly what he has said (Numbers 30:2 Msg).

COMMENTARY

A vow is a promise, pledge, or personal commitment. I mentioned in an earlier devotion my mom's saying, "Your word is your bond." It is an important part of your integrity to honor your promises. If something happens and you can't keep your promise, be honest about it. Confess that you thought you could do it, but you can't. When you don't keep commitments, you waste other people's time, so be honest. Most important, don't break your vows/promises to God. Think and pray before you make commitments to the Lord. We should never make promises lightly. Go before the Lord, and if He leads you to do it, do so with His guidance and be steadfast. That is an important characteristic of a good businessperson. God bless.

What vows have you broken to God? Confess them now.

_____

_____

_____

_____

_____

_____

_____

177. The Excitement of Serving Others

Good morning entrepreneurs,

The thief comes only in order to steal and kill and destroy. I came that they may have and enjoy life, and have it in abundance [to the full, till it overflows] (John 10:10 AMP).

I have discovered that the abundant life begins when you serve others. In your business, your church, your personal life, on the street with a stranger, there are always opportunities to serve. Christ lived a life of service to others. He never turned away from an opportunity to serve others. As we strive to be more like Christ, we must do the same. Remember we do not serve so we can receive; we serve out of obedience to God. God bless.

How can you serve someone today?

_____

_____

_____

_____

_____

_____

_____

_____

_____

_____

_____

178. Watch the Lord Fight for You

Good morning entrepreneurs,

For the Lord your God is the One who goes with you to fight for you against your enemies to give you victory (Deuteronomy 20:4 NIV).

COMMENTARY

Whether you are having problems in your business or your personal life, you want someone you can go to when you need help. It wasn't until later in my life I discovered the magnitude of the scripture above. Something happened that almost devastated my life. So, I said, "I'm going to trust you Lord and believe this scripture is true." When I tell you that my life and my business changed when I stopped trying to talk my way through my battles and sincerely gave them to God, He completely changed my marriage, my finances, my business, and my perspective on life. I recommend you memorize this scripture, let it get into your mind and your spirit, follow what it says, and believe it is true. You will see a change in your life. God bless.

What did God reveal to you through today's devotion?

_____

_____

_____

_____

_____

_____

_____

179. The "Present" of Today

Good morning entrepreneurs,

This [day in which God has saved me] is the day which the Lord has made. Let us rejoice and be glad in it (Psalm 118:24 AMP).

COMMENTARY

As we move toward the end of this devotional journey, it is important to remember that each day we wake up is a present from God. When you open your eyes, give thanks that God has given you another day to do His work, and be joyful! God bless.

What will you do with today's "Present" from God?

_____

_____

_____

_____

_____

_____

_____

_____

_____

_____

_____

_____

180. Plans and Actions

Good morning entrepreneurs,

The plans and reflections of the heart belong to man, but the [wise] answer of the tongue is from the Lord. All the ways of a man are clean and innocent in his own eyes [and he may see nothing wrong with his actions], but the Lord weighs and examines the motives and intents [of the heart and knows the truth]. Commit your works to the Lord [submit and trust them to Him], and your plans will succeed [if you respond to His will and guidance] (Proverbs 16:1-3 AMP).

COMMENTARY

Today's devotion is an important reminder. Plans and actions work together. If you have plans but no actions, your business will remain stagnate (not moving and not growing). If you have actions but no plan, you will be running in many different directions but accomplishing nothing. The plan must come first. Then each action will lead you toward the goal of success. Never forget that the motivation for what you do is known by God, for He knows your heart. Begin with right motivation, then the plan and action will be right. Each time you take a step, remember to ask God to show you what is next. God bless.

What is the motivation for your plans and actions?

_____

_____

_____

_____

_____

_____

181. How to Involve God in Your Life

Good morning entrepreneurs,

God wants us to spend time with Him! In fact, the more time we spend with God, the more He will be involved in our lives (James 4:8 NIV).

COMMENTARY

If we want the Lord to be number one in our life, we must spend adequate time with Him. Focusing on the five areas below can help us live according to God's purposes:

1. Our top priority should be spending time with the Lord each day. We can read and meditate on His Word, pray, listen for His directions, or simply be with Him.

2. We should allot time to family and friends, since Galatians 6:2 (NIV) says "Carry each other's burdens and in this way, you will fulfill the law of Christ."

3. The area most likely to become imbalanced is our work. The Lord disapproves of laziness, but He doesn't want us to be overly consumed with our careers, either.

4. It's vital to take care of our body, allocating adequate time for rest, recreation, and exercise.

5. The Scriptures urge to meet together regularly with other believers for worship (Heb. 10:24-25).

These general areas all need space in your life, but I can't tell you how each day should look. Ask the Lord to direct your time with Him. Seek His guidance, watch for His answers, and make the changes He brings to mind. God bless.

What did God reveal to you through today's devotion?

_____

_____

_____

_____

_____

_____

_____

_____

_____

_____

_____

_____

_____

_____

_____

_____

_____

_____

_____

_____

182. The Importance of Beginning Your Day with Prayer

Good morning entrepreneurs,

In the morning, O Lord, You will hear my voice. In the morning I will prepare [a prayer and a sacrifice] for You and watch and wait [for You to speak to my heart] (Psalm 5:3 AMP).

COMMENTARY

How are you doing with beginning your day with prayer? This was expressed before, but is important to fine tune in this 4th phase. The above scripture reinforces how important it is. As a businessperson, starting our day with prayer is essential! As we develop our business, we must allow God to guide us. God is waiting for us early in the morning. Listen for instructions for the day then be obedient. God bless.

How early is the Lord leading you to get up for prayer?

_____

_____

_____

_____

_____

_____

_____

_____

_____

183. Don't Allow Frustrations to Consume You

Good morning entrepreneurs,

Haven't I commanded you? Strength! Courage! Don't be timid; don't get discouraged. God, your God, is with you every step you take (Joshua 1:9 MS).

COMMENTARY

What is your customer's pain?

We are in business to help resolve someone's pain and minister to them through our product/services. We know how to apply and believe the above scripture for our lives. This scripture is shared today to focus on your customers. Meditate on and ask yourself the following:

1. What pain or frustration does my product or service address?

2. How will it resolve my customer's pain or frustration?

3. How do I find the customers whose pain my product or service can resolve?

4. Am I ready to do all I can to help them?

Let's take time today to set aside our own fears, anxiety, and discouragement to focus on our customers and how our product/services can help them. God bless.

What did God reveal to you through today's devotion?

_____

_____

_____

_____

184. Your Words Have Power

Good morning entrepreneurs,

For by your words you will be acquitted, and by your words you will be condemned (Matthew 12:37).

COMMENTARY

Do you believe what you say? Do you believe nothing is impossible with God? Do you believe our plan happens in God's timing? Do you believe everything in our lives work together for the good? What you say with your mouth (good or bad) can become reality. Say what you believe and believe what you say! Watch your words, they have power. God bless.

What did God reveal to you through today's devotion?

_____

_____

_____

_____

_____

_____

_____

_____

_____

_____

_____

185. Which Path is God's Path?

Good morning entrepreneurs,
Urging you on whenever you wander left or right: "This is the right road. Walk down this road" (Isaiah 30:21 MSG).

COMMENTARY

When you act on the decisions you make for your business, do you hear a little voice say, "Yes move forward in this" or "No don't do that" or "Wait, don't move yet?" Do you listen to that voice, or do you continue with your plans your way? That small voice is the Holy Spirit guiding you. Ignoring it will lead you down the wrong path. We like to think that we are in charge of our life's decisions. We are, in that we make the choice on who to follow, our mind or God's. Even in that, ultimately it is God who is in charge of our decisions and how those decisions affect us.

To make godly decisions, we must learn to know the Holy Spirit's voice and be obedient to it. Then we know no matter what the decision is, God is with us, and it will be for our good. God bless.

What did God reveal to you through today's devotion?

_____

_____

_____

_____

_____

_____

_____

186. The Devastation of Distractions

Good morning entrepreneurs,

Keep your eyes straight ahead; ignore all sideshow distractions (Proverbs 4:25 MSG).

COMMENTARY

One last word on distractions! There are so many people and things to take us off our path for success that I don't have room to list them all! The distractions are different for each of us. If we are to avoid being distracted, we must know the triggers to our distractions and ask the Lord for strength, so we are not diverted from the path He has for us.

Spend some time today identifying things and people who distract you. Next, pray for God's discernment to overcome and continue walking the straight path to God's destiny for your life. God bless.

What is your biggest distraction? How have these devotions helped you to improve?

_____

_____

_____

_____

_____

_____

_____

_____

187. How to Love Your Enemies

Good morning entrepreneurs,

To you who are ready for the truth, I say this: Love your enemies. Let them bring out the best in you, not the worst. When someone gives you a hard time, respond with the energies of prayer for that person (Luke 6:27-28 MSG).

COMMENTARY

In business and in our personal lives, we will encounter people who we feel only want to see us suffer or want to say and do hurtful things to us. Sometimes they are the people who are closest to us. We don't want to consider them enemies, but they are. They are enemies in that they are hindrances to our journey. We can only live out the above scriptures by asking God to help us. Let our enemies bring out the best in us and respond in prayer for those that give us a hard time. We cannot attain that character on our own! It means not saying what we want to say, but what God tells us to say (or saying nothing) and praying silently through the situation. It is a difficult command to obey, but with God nothing is impossible. God bless.

What did God reveal to you through today's devotion?

_____

_____

_____

_____

_____

_____

_____

188. God's Forgiveness When We Fall Short

Good morning entrepreneurs,

If we [freely] admit that we have sinned and confess our sins, He is faithful and just [true to His own nature and promises] and will forgive our sins and cleanse us continually from all unrighteousness [our wrongdoing, everything not in conformity with His will and purpose] (1 John 1:9 AMP).

COMMENTARY

Sometimes we feel like we have fallen short in our business and that we should be further along with developing it. When we think like that, we can get discouraged. We should not be weighed down by guilt. The scripture above tells us that if we admit our sin to God of falling short in our business and purpose, He will forgive us. Don't spend time thinking about what you should have done, ask for forgiveness. If you are reading this devotion, you still have time to do it! God bless.

What did God reveal to you through today's devotion?

_____

_____

_____

_____

_____

_____

_____

_____

_____

189. Do You Have the Mind of a Businessperson or an Entrepreneur?

Good morning entrepreneurs,

I have filled him with the Spirit of God in wisdom and skill, in understanding and intelligence, in knowledge, and in all kinds of craftsmanship, to make artistic designs for work in gold, in silver, and in bronze, and in the cutting of stones for settings, and in the carving of wood, to work in all kinds of craftsmanship (Exodus 31:3-5 AMP).

COMMENTARY

Businessman Vs Entrepreneur

A businessman is someone who sets up a business with an existing idea, offering products and services to the customers. An entrepreneur is a person who starts an enterprise with a new idea or concept, undertaking commercial activities (S, Surbhi. "Key Differences," May 3, 2023. As men and women of God, we want to be entrepreneurs.

As you meditate on the above, ask the Lord to show you if you are a businessperson or an entrepreneur. God bless.

What did God reveal to you through today's devotion?

_____

_____

_____

_____

_____

_____

190. Mentoring is Reciprocal

Good morning entrepreneurs,
Save your breath for the wise - they'll be wiser for it; tell good people what you know - they'll profit from it (Proverbs 9:9 MSG).

COMMENTARY

A mentor is someone who teaches or gives help and advice to a less experienced and often younger person. We should all have a mentor. Someone who is spiritually wise, wise in business and has (or had) a business of their own. If you don't have a mentor, prayerfully ask the Lord to show you who He wants to be your mentor and then ask them. The following two sites can provide more insight into understanding what a mentor is and how to find one:

D'Angelo, Matt. "How to Find a Mentor." Business News Daily, February 21, 2023. www.businessnewsdaily.com.

Cronin, Nicola, Guider, February 16, 2022. www.guider-ai.com.

In the same way, we should also be a mentor to someone, teaching them how God has guided us and sharing our wisdom and skills with them. Don't wait until you are successful in the eyes of the world. As your business grows, you have wisdom to share at each level. Have a mentor and be a mentor! God bless.

What did God reveal to you through today's devotion?

_____

_____

_____

_____

191. Avoiding Those Who Work Against You

Good morning entrepreneurs,
Christ has set us free to live a free life. So, take your stand! Never again let anyone put a harness of slavery on you (Galatians 5:1 MSG).

COMMENTARY

Has anyone attempted to hinder you from living the life God ordained you to live? Accusing you of things? Putting restrictions on you? Perhaps it was someone telling you that you don't have what it takes to start a business. Maybe it is your own mind saying, "I am not good enough or smart enough." Because of Christ's death and resurrection, He has given us the freedom to do impossible things! We are no longer slaves to anyone or anything (even the thoughts in our own mind)! Allow your freedom in Christ to give you the strength to pursue your gift in business! God bless.

What did God reveal to you through today's devotion?

_____

_____

_____

_____

_____

_____

_____

_____

_____

192. The Pitfalls of Fatigue

Good morning entrepreneurs,

For the one who has once entered His rest has also rested from [the weariness and pain of] his [human] labors, just as God rested from [those labors uniquely] His own. Let us therefore make every effort to enter that rest [of God, to know and experience it for ourselves], so that no one will fall by following the same example of disobedience [as those who died in the wilderness] (Hebrews 4:10-11 AMP).

COMMENTARY

Overworking in anything causes fatigue. Do you find yourself feeling tired? Burned out? Frustrated? We must have time to replenish our bodies and our minds. God rested one day each week; do we follow His example? Plan one day a week when you do not work. Try to plan one day each month to do something different or take a short trip. It will replenish your soul. God bless.

What did God reveal to you through today's devotion?

_____

_____

_____

_____

_____

_____

_____

_____

_____

193. Becoming God's Representative

Good morning entrepreneurs,

So, we are ambassadors for Christ, as though God were making His appeal through us; we [as Christ's representatives] plead with you on behalf of Christ to be reconciled to God (2 Corinthians 5:20 AMP).

COMMENTARY

As godly men and women, we are God's representatives, whether we want to or not. Everything we do or say can potentially lead someone to or away from Christ. Our business gives us a unique opportunity. God will send people to us, not just to purchase our products or services, but to encourage, minister, and pray with. Always be ready to share your experiences with others and to encourage them to have a relationship with Christ. God bless.

What did God reveal to you through today's devotion?

_____

_____

_____

_____

_____

_____

_____

_____

_____

_____

194. Allow God to Be Your Business Consultant

Good morning entrepreneurs,

What's God going to say to my questions? I'm braced for the worst. I'll climb to the lookout tower and scan the horizon. I'll wait to see what God says, how he'll answer my complaint. And then God answered: 'Write this. Write what you see. Write it out in big block letters so that it can be read on the run' (Habakkuk 2:1-2 MSG).

COMMENTARY

What questions have you asked the Lord about your business? Has He answered you? If so, did you write them down? God's answers to your questions about your business are your blueprint! Have you written it yet? Write it out in a form so you can read it on the run! Smartsheet website has a one-page business template you can use, which is cited under the resource section of this book. God bless.

What did God reveal to you through today's devotion?

_____

_____

_____

_____

_____

_____

_____

_____

_____

_____

195. Selfishness Does Not Honor God

Good morning entrepreneurs,

Do nothing from selfishness or empty conceit [through factional motives, or strife], but with [an attitude of] humility [being neither arrogant nor self-righteous], regard others as more important than yourselves (Philippians 2:3 AMP).

COMMENTARY

As our business begins to grow and the income increases, we may be tempted to brag about what "We" have done. It is okay to graciously accept compliments, but do not forget to give God the glory for the success of your business. These are opportunities to testify not to brag. Also, remember to be a blessing to those who helped you along the way (including your customers). As the scripture commands, "Regard others more important than yourself," even when you are successful. God bless.

What did God reveal to you through today's devotion?

_____

_____

_____

_____

_____

_____

_____

_____

196. Be Ready for the Changing Seasons

Good morning entrepreneurs,

There's an opportune time to do things, a right time for everything on the earth (Ecclesiastes 3:1 MSG).

COMMENTARY

One of my favorite sayings is, "Things can change in the blink of an eye." Just when we think we have settled into a routine, something happens that changes everything! The only thing that doesn't change is God's love for and protection of us. He will lead and guide us through every situation we encounter if we trust Him.

What did God reveal to you through today's devotion?

_____

_____

_____

_____

_____

_____

_____

_____

_____

_____

_____

197. Dress for Success

Good morning entrepreneurs,

In conclusion, be strong in the Lord [draw your strength from Him and be empowered through your union with Him] and in the power of His [boundless] might. Put on the full armor of God [for His precepts are like the splendid armor of a heavily armed soldier], so that you may be able to [successfully] stand up against all the schemes and the strategies and the deceits of the devil. For our struggle is not against flesh and blood [contending only with physical opponents], but against the rulers, against the powers, against the world forces of this [present] darkness, against the spiritual forces of wickedness in the heavenly (supernatural) places. Therefore, put on the complete armor of God, so that you will be able to [successfully] resist and stand your ground in the evil day [of danger], and having done everything [that the crisis demands], to stand firm [in your place, fully prepared, immovable, victorious] (Ephesians 6:10-13 AMP).

COMMENTARY

The world says we must dress for success, that our outward appearance affects people's first impression of us. As an etiquette consultant, I agree with that statement, but it is much more important to dress for battle with the evil of this world. Putting on the whole armor of God arms you with the Lord's protection during the day. After dressing in the armor, ask the Lord, "What should I wear today that will give you glory?" Dress for battle first! God bless.

What did God reveal to you through today's devotion?

_____

_____

_____

_____

198. The Walls of Your Business

Good morning entrepreneurs,

Then Hezekiah turned his face to the wall and prayed to the LORD, AND said, "Please, O LORD, just remember how I have walked before You in faithfulness and truth, and with a whole heart [absolutely devoted to You] and have done what is good in Your sight." And Hezekiah wept greatly. Then the word of the LORD came to Isaiah, saying, "Go and say to Hezekiah, 'For the LORD, the God of David your father says this, "I have heard your prayer, I have seen your tears; listen carefully, I will add fifteen years to your life"' (Isaiah 38:2-5 AMP).

COMMENTARY

Do you pray within the walls of your business? Do you walk around the space and bring to God's remembrance your obedience and how you have strived to walk faithfully in His ways? Has God sent godly counsel to you to affirm that He is going to bless you? Did you receive what you were told? Anoint the walls of your business and claim the success of your business in the name of Jesus. God bless.

What did God reveal to you through today's devotion?

_____

_____

_____

_____

_____

_____

_____

199. The Overwhelming Desire

Good morning entrepreneurs,
Delight yourself in the LORD, *and He will give you the desires and petitions of your* heart (Psalm 37:4 AMP).

COMMENTARY

We all have desires. Things we want that are beyond what we need. The question is, are those desires in line with God's will and plan for our lives? They absolutely may be, but did you seek the Lord? I have always wanted to see the Arora Borealis (Northern Lights). The best place to see them is in Iceland. This was obviously a desire, not a need. As my 70th birthday approached, I had really let go of the idea because my finances would not allow me to make a trip like that. On Thanksgiving Day 2022, my son, and his fiancée told me that for my 70th birthday, my son is taking me to Iceland to see the Northern Lights! I share this with you to say, God will give you the desires of your heart if they are in line with His will for you and you truly believe, and you may not even see how it will happen. God bless.

What did God reveal to you through today's devotion?

_____

_____

_____

_____

_____

_____

_____

200. A Spirit of Gratefulness

Good morning entrepreneurs,
In every situation [no matter what the circumstances] be thankful and continually give thanks to God; for this is the will of God for you in Christ Jesus (1 Thessalonians 5:18 AMP).

COMMENTARY

Life is not perfect. Every day we encounter problems, issues, setbacks, and disappointments. Some days are easier than others, but there are always decisions to make. Once we understand that God is the head of our life, and He is in control of everything and everyone, life becomes a little easier. Why? Because we understand that we must be grateful for the blessings and the trials. The trials test and teach us, while the blessings give us joy. As children of God, we must live in a lifestyle of gratefulness. In our personal life and our business, God is in control, and nothing happens to us that He does not allow. For that we must be grateful! God bless.

What did God reveal to you through today's devotion?

_____

_____

_____

_____

_____

_____

_____

201. A Word About Multi-Tasking

Good morning entrepreneurs,
One hand full of rest and patience is better than two fists full of labor and chasing after the wind (Ecclesiastes 4:6 AMP).

COMMENTARY

I remember years ago my pastor preached a sermon about "Too Many Things in Hand." The next morning, I was walking from my car to my office and both hands were full. As I walked, I thought, "I have too many things in my hands. I am doing too much. Lord, help me let go of the things I need to let go of." Those of us who are multitaskers like to boast about it. It is a good attribute, but when is it too much? My mom used to say, "If you have too many balls in the air at once, they will all fall." As entrepreneurs, we juggle many balls. We must be careful, though, not to burn ourselves out. We can't be all things to all people, and God doesn't want us to. Ask God to prioritize your multitasking and show you what things to let go of. When God orders your steps, you will be an efficient multitasker! God bless.

What did God reveal to you through today's devotion?

_____

_____

_____

_____

_____

_____

_____

202. Know Your Limits

Good morning entrepreneurs,

I have seen that all [human] perfection has its limits [no matter how grand and perfect and noble]; Your commandment is exceedingly broad and extends without limits [into eternity] I have seen that all [human] perfection has its limits [no matter how grand and perfect and noble]; Your commandment is exceedingly broad and extends without limits [into eternity] (Psalm 119:96 AMP).

COMMENTARY

We have a saying in our church to "Stay in your lane." Know your limits not only with your gifts, but with what you should do in life. Know when to say no to something that is outside of your expertise. Learn to say no when God tells you it is time to rest. Learn to say no when God says it is time to let go of a job, or even a responsibility at church, or in your business. As we get older, understand your physical limits and be mindful of them. You should even know your limits as to your health. We are all bound by limits in our lives. Knowing those limits and being obedient to what God tells us about living within those limits will result in a more joyful and fruitful life. God bless.

What did God reveal to you through today's devotion?

_____

_____

_____

_____

_____

_____

203. Look Before You Leap

Good morning entrepreneurs,
He who answers before he hears [the facts]—It is folly and shame to him (Proverbs 18:13 AMP).

COMMENTARY

I want to be transparent in this devotion. I used to be an impulsive person (I still can be, if not careful). I didn't even realize it was a spirit of impulsivity. If something looked good, I bought it and did not consider the consequences. If I wanted to do something, I did it. Again, not worrying about the consequences. When God gave me the idea for my business, I wanted to jump right in, but I couldn't. I didn't have the finances I needed because of bad financial decisions in the past. So, I prayed for God to show me how to start the business I knew He was calling me to. I prayed daily for God to remove the spirit of impulsivity in my life and teach me how to seek Him before doing anything. God has answered my prayers. I'm not completely healed, but now I look, stop, pray, then slowly walk (which gives God time to pull me back if I should not do it) not leap. God bless.

What did God reveal to you through today's devotion?

_____

_____

_____

_____

_____

_____

204. Be Careful of Envy

Good morning entrepreneurs,

Do not let your heart envy sinners [who live godless lives and have no hope of salvation], But [continue to] live in the [reverent, worshipful] fear of the Lord day by day (Proverbs 23:17 AMP).

COMMENTARY

We tend to look at what others have and, even though we don't intend to, we become envious. If you are reading this devotion, God has blessed you with a business or an idea for a business. That gift is not given to everyone, so be grateful. Remember God has a different plan for you. Rejoice in His plan for you and bind that spirit of envy! God bless.

What did God reveal to you through today's devotion?

_____

_____

_____

_____

_____

_____

_____

_____

_____

_____

205. Go Ye Therefore

Good morning entrepreneurs,

Listen carefully: we are going up to Jerusalem; and the Son of Man will be handed over to the chief priests and scribes (Sanhedrin, Jewish High Court), and they will [judicially] condemn Him and sentence Him to death (Matthew 20:18 AMP).

COMMENTARY

"Go ye therefore." "Enlarge your territory." These are excerpts from familiar scriptures encouraging us to keep moving forward. Being in business opens so many doors. It may provide opportunities for speaking engagements, mentorships, teaching, helping those in need and much more. The idea God gave us for our business provides a platform for us to reach out to others and give a testimony to those whose level of faith may need increasing. Pray, then take the opportunities God puts before you to spread His Word and His goodness to others.

What did God reveal to you through today's devotion?

_____

_____

_____

_____

_____

_____

_____

_____

206. You Can Do All Things

Good morning entrepreneurs,

I can do all things [which He has called me to do] through Him who strengthens and empowers me [to fulfill His purpose—I am self-sufficient in Christ's sufficiency; I am ready for anything and equal to anything through Him who infuses me with inner strength and confident peace] (Philippians 4:13 AMP).

COMMENTARY

I didn't think I could begin a consulting business, have a stressful career, raise two children, have a husband, a household to run, publish three books, and be active in my church. I was right! I could not do it, **BUT GOD!** When I became overwhelmed, anxious, and afraid, I said, "God I can't do all of this!" His answer was, "Lean on me and I will provide what you need to fulfill your calling." All you need is the willingness to be obedient to what God is leading you to do and **He** will give you the strength, knowledge, and wisdom to do what He has called you to do. It is not about what you can do, but what you can do through Christ Jesus to glorify Him!

What did God reveal to you through today's devotion?

_____

_____

_____

_____

_____

_____

_____

207. God is in the Center

Good morning entrepreneurs,

Whatever you do [no matter what it is] in word or deed, do everything in the name of the Lord Jesus [and in dependence on Him], giving thanks to God the Father through Him (Colossians 3:17 AMP).

COMMENTARY

Where does God fit in your business? Were you prayerful in the startup of your business but now you believe you can handle it yourself? Do you go to God only when things become difficult, and you have nowhere else to turn? If your business is going to be successful and reach the people God has envisioned it to, He must be in the center of it. Every morning, before every decision, before greeting any customer, ask God to lead and guide you. The center is the nucleus, and the all the other parts are around it. God must be the nucleus of your business.

What did God reveal to you through today's devotion?

_____

_____

_____

_____

_____

_____

_____

_____

_____

208. God is Your Partner

Good morning entrepreneurs,

He who watches the wind [waiting for all conditions to be perfect] will not sow [seed], and he who looks at the clouds will not reap [a harvest] (Ecclesiastes 11:4 AMP).

COMMENTARY

Your business ultimately belongs to God. If He is telling you to move but you are waiting for more financing, more customers, it is the same as waiting for everything to be perfect. We know that God does not work in perfect conditions. As a matter of fact, it is usually when things are at the worst or lowest point that He acts. Don't operate your business with your head in the clouds waiting for the "Perfect" opportunity. You sow the most when circumstances make your situation look the least likely to succeed. When God sends customers, don't look for the most lucrative one. Look closer and follow God's direction for a harvest beyond measure. God bless.

What did God reveal to you through today's devotion?

_____

_____

_____

_____

_____

_____

_____

209. Launch into the Deep

Good morning entrepreneurs,
When He had finished speaking, He said to Simon [Peter], "Put out into the deep water and lower your nets for a catch [of fish]" (Luke 5:4 AMP).

COMMENTARY

You have stepped out of the boat to either start your business, or you are in it already, but hesitant about moving to the next level. In the scripture above, Peter and his fellow fishermen had been fishing all night and caught nothing. They were not fishing for sport; this was their livelihood, so they knew what they were doing. When Jesus told Peter to launch into the deep and lower his net "for a catch of fish," He was not just telling Peter what to do, He was telling him what the result would be! Peter trusted Jesus and was obedient. The catch they made was so large that their nets were at the point of breaking and other fishermen had to come and help. So, what are you waiting for? Launch out to do what God has shown you and be ready for a "Catch" beyond your wildest expectations! God bless.

What did God reveal to you through today's devotion?

_____

_____

_____

_____

_____

_____

210. God is Amazing!

Good morning entrepreneurs,

Great is our [majestic and mighty] Lord and abundant in strength;
His understanding is inexhaustible [infinite, boundless] (Psalm 147:5 AMP).

COMMENTARY

How great is our God! He is omnipotent (infinite in power), omniscient (unlimited knowledge), and omnipresent (everywhere at the same time). He is loving, forgiving, and compassionate. He is our protector, healer, guide, and provider. Knowing this gives us just a glimpse as to how amazing God is. For today's devotion, let's just praise God for how amazing He is!

What did God reveal to you through today's devotion?

_____

_____

_____

_____

_____

_____

_____

_____

_____

_____

211. Be Like a Tree

Good morning entrepreneurs,

Blessed [fortunate, prosperous, and favored by God] is the man who does not walk in the counsel of the wicked [following their advice and example], Nor stand in the path of sinners, nor sit [down to rest] in the seat of scoffers (ridiculers). But his delight is in the law of the LORD, and on His law [His precepts and teachings] he [habitually] meditates day and night. and he will be like a tree firmly planted [and fed] by streams of water, which yields its fruit in its season; Its leaf does not wither; And in whatever he does, he prospers (Psalm 1:1-3 AMP).

COMMENTARY

As I take my daily walk, I look at the trees in our neighborhood. They are so strong, so majestic. They have been standing for hundreds of years. They have survived rainstorms, hurricanes and snowstorms, tsunamis, earthquakes, and much more. In some areas, where the seasons change, the leaves die. When we delight in the Lord and in His Word, we will be like trees, firmly planted, fed by the water of His Word, and yielding fruit in our season. Plant yourself in and be watered by the Word. Do not allow discouragement or disappointments to make you shrivel or decay. Then, whatever you do will prosper as you come into your season. God bless.

What did God reveal to you through today's devotion?

_____

_____

_____

_____

_____

212. You Have the Power of God in You

Good morning entrepreneurs,

But you will receive power and ability when the Holy Spirit comes upon you; and you will be My witnesses [to tell people about Me] both in Jerusalem and in all Judea, and Samaria, and even to the ends of the earth (Acts 1:8 AMP).

COMMENTARY

You have the power within you to do whatever God calls you to do. That power is manifested in the Holy Spirit. It is not a loud voice but a still soft voice. The power is not given to you just for your success but to allow what God blesses you with to be able to help others. Power is defined as "The ability to do or to act" (2018 *Dictionary.com*, LLC). God's power is infinite and limitless. Remember, with God's power you can do anything but fail. Tap into God's power and be led by the power of the Holy Spirit for the success of your business and to be a witness to tell others how they may obtain God's power. God bless.

What did God reveal to you through today's devotion?

_____

_____

_____

_____

_____

_____

_____

213. Every Day is a New Day

Good morning entrepreneurs,

It is because of the LORD's loving kindnesses that we are not consumed, Because His [tender] compassions never fail. They are new every morning; Great and beyond measure is Your faithfulness (Lamentations 3:22-23 AMP).

COMMENTARY

New things: they may be daunting (scary or intimidating). They may cause anxiety or impatience to know what will happen. I challenge you to not focus on the past; Look for the new things God is doing in your life. I can tell you new things from God, if you allow them, will bring excitement, joy, peace, new revelations, strength. Most of all, each "new thing" you allow God to do in your life will draw you closer to your relationship with Him. Embrace the newness! God bless.

What did God reveal to you through today's devotion?

_____

_____

_____

_____

_____

_____

_____

_____

_____

_____

214. Walking in Your Newness

Good morning entrepreneurs,

Listen carefully, I am about to do a new thing, now it will spring forth. Will you not be aware of it? I will even put a road in the wilderness, Rivers in the desert (Isaiah 43:19 AMP).

COMMENTARY

What "new thing" is God about to birth in you during this season? During this time of drawing closer to God, ask Him to show you what it is. Perhaps it is a new product or service for your business or a new marketing strategy. Maybe even opportunities for speaking engagements. The possibilities are endless! Be intentional in praying and claiming, in the name of Jesus, that God will reveal the "new thing" in you, and it will "spring forth." God bless.

How will you "Spring forth" in your new godly entrepreneurial spirit? Write Down the steps you will follow.

_____

_____

_____

_____

_____

_____

_____

_____

_____

215. Will You Trust God?

Good morning entrepreneurs,

The LORD is my strength and my [impenetrable] shield; My heart trusts [with unwavering confidence] in Him, and I am helped; Therefore, my heart greatly rejoices, and with my song I shall thank Him and praise Him (Psalm 28:7 AMP).

COMMENTARY

As we come to the last day of this seven-month devotional, I have one question for you, "Will you trust God?" The journey to write these devotionals has taken me almost two years. I didn't even realize that it was a book, as I believed I was simply being obedient to God to send encouraging scriptures and messages to members of my church's business ministry. We must always remember that as a child of God, we never know why He is leading us to do things, and we don't really need to know. Our job is to be obedient. So, on this last day of this journey, I will encourage you to trust God. Whatever you believe He is leading you to do, be obedient. If you start on the wrong path, He will turn you around while teaching and strengthening you. Don't be afraid; trust God!! God bless.

Use this page to summarize your seven-month journey. What did you learn and how have you transformed during this journey? What do you need to do to remain on course with the Lord and with your business?

_____

_____

_____

_____

_____

_____

_____

_____

_____

_____

_____

_____

_____

_____

_____

_____

_____

_____

_____

Resource Page

BUSINESS PLAN LINK

https://www.smartsheet.com/sites/default/files/2020-10/IC-One-Page-Business-Plan-10787_PDF.pdf

TO DO LIST LINK

https://www.smartsheet.com/15-free-task-list-templates

INCOME/EXPENSE SHEET LINK:

https://template.wps.com/excel/income-expenditure-75/

About the Author

Linda J. Williams has dedicated over 25 years of her life to helping others. Her credentials as a Certified Etiquette Consultant, Certified Book Coach, author, speaker, and ministry leader with a Bachelor of Science Degree in Sociology and a Master of Arts in Education validate her knowledge and wisdom. Her goal is to help others discover and grow in their purpose to bring God glory.

To contact the author or schedule a speaking engagement, please visit her website at www.etiquetteandwritingconsultancy.com.

www.ingramcontent.com/pod-product-compliance
Lightning Source LLC
Chambersburg PA
CBHW071154130626
46553CB00004B/1653